A LABORATORY FOR
ECUMENICAL LIFE

A LABORATORY FOR ECUMENICAL LIFE

THE STORY OF BOSSEY
1946-1996

Hans-Ruedi Weber

WCC Publications, Geneva

Cover design: Edwin Hassink
Cover photo: Peter Williams/WCC

ISBN 2-8254-1215-5

© 1996 WCC Publications, World Council of Churches,
150 route de Ferney, 1211 Geneva 2, Switzerland

Printed in Switzerland

Table of Contents

Preface

A source of living water?

The small fountain of the château de Bossey cannot of course compare with the Jet d'Eau, the impressive fountain which is Geneva's landmark, or with the glorious fountains of the city of Rome. The Ecumenical Institute too plays only a small role in the worldwide movement which draws Christians and churches together for renewing their life in order to worship, witness and serve more credibly in the world. Nevertheless, those who participate in meetings at Bossey often find there the true water of life.

On clear days when the sprinkling drops of the fountain shine and sparkle, they vividly symbolize the excitement experienced when people from many nations meet, discuss their own and the world's problems, seek new insights and grow together into a fuller life. There are also days when the fountain is dry, when despite all the talk and work little happens at the Institute. Or the falling water may only symbolize the endless succession of words, words and ever more words in the hundreds of conferences and courses which take place here. Bossey knows years of plenty and years of scarcity, hours of excitement and long arid days when nothing really happens.

This story is told in the first place for the thousands of people who came from around the world to join in a common search. These former participants — and those who come today — will remember only what they experienced at a given time and with a particular group. They may want to know more about other moments of truth, tension, discovery, pain and joy during the fifty years of life at Bossey. What was the vision that inspired the pioneers? What was it like to be at the Institute in the late 1940s? What changes took place in the following decades when ever more participants came not only from the Western world but also from Asia, Africa, Latin America and the Pacific Islands? How did the student revolts in the late 1960s affect the life and teaching at the Institute? How did Bossey survive the monetary crisis in the 1970s and initiate a new ministry for responding to the challenges of the last decades of the 20th century?

In this chronicle readers arc first introduced to the place itself and the worldwide fellowship of Bossey (ch. 1). They will meet some of the persons who were responsible for, and a few movements that led to, the creation of the Institute (ch. 2). Following this, the main periods in the fifty-year history of the Institute are sketched (chs 3-6). Bossey has often been called an "ecumenical laboratory". Its discoveries and failures, its experience of community life and worship as well as the subjects chosen for teaching and learning can perhaps serve as an ecumenical case study. Many of the insights gained are summed up in published or multicopied reports still buried in the archives (see appendix C), and these may well be of interest to those who wish to learn from the lessons of history.

The story is dedicated to the children from many nations who grew up at Bossey, and among them Marc, a boy not yet two years old when he lost his life in the pond on one of his voyages of discovery around the château. Children have not figured prominently in the studies at the Ecumenical Institute. Yet adults exploring here so many serious questions of human life could have much to learn from the curiosity of little boys and girls, and the joy they have and the risks they take to discover new things.

Pentecost 1996   H.-R.W.

1. Introducing Bossey

Bossey evokes different things to different people. Its story should not be told just by one person but by a whole group of participants at meetings of the Ecumenical Institute and by staff members who lived there for many years. During a cold winter evening such a group could sit in front of the fireplace in the *Salon blanc*, the white lounge of the château. On a hot summer day they might prefer the garden chairs and sit in a circle under the large chestnut trees near the old, round tower. Together they could then remember, listen and talk, each contributing her or his own part of the story.

A place to remember

The region of Bossey is indeed a place to remember. Coming by car from Geneva or from the railway station at Céligny, one sees the long range of the Jura mountains: peaceful ridges with large pine forests and pastures about ten kilometers to the north-west, no higher than 1600 metres. In all seasons of the year this is ideal country for walking, perhaps most beautiful in autumn with all the changing colours, or for cross-country skiing on a sunny winter day, looking down on the sea of fog and clouds which often at that time cover the Geneva region. Approaching Bossey, one comes to winding narrow roads through a lovely, park-like landscape, with meadows and large trees, and an occasional farm.

Entering the domain of Bossey there is a stately country house with a barn: "Petit Bossey". It belongs to the Institute and many participants of courses and conferences have stayed here. A five-minute walk towards the lake, and one enters the courtyard of the château. Not one of those massive stone castles on top of a rocky hill, but simply a large, 18th-century three-floor mansion, set in the midst of meadows, with a pond opposite the entrance. Through the trees one sees a few modern buildings: the lecture hall and the library. Between the château and the lecture hall is the volley-ball court. After hours of reading and heated discussions covering all things under the sun, there is nothing more refreshing than a vigorous game!

More will be said later about the château itself, its history and present role. Passing through the entry hall and out again one is struck by the beauty of the south-eastern front: the long main facade of the château with wisteria climbing high up, facing a large lawn, old chestnut trees bordering it on both sides and the small fountain in the middle. To the left stands a large, single-storeyed building, the "Orangerie". It was used by a former owner as a museum for his collection of paintings and now serves as the dining hall and lounge, a long string of roses creeping up the wall between the large windows. To the right of the lawn is a garden path, sheltered by pear trees, which leads to the houses of the teaching staff. Towards the south-east is a hedge low enough to see what lies beyond.

The view from the château is striking: nearby meadows and vineyards gradually slope down to Lake Geneva. From the porter's small picturesque house a straight alley, bordered by trees, leads right down to the lake. On clear days the whole range of the Alps appears beyond. Those who hope to get a glimpse of the majestic Mont Blanc will be disappointed; from here the highest mountain of Europe is almost totally hidden by the pre-Alps of Savoy.

What impress most visitors immediately are *the old tower and the chapel* near the Orangerie. Only this 12th-century round tower remains of the medieval complex, and it functions as the landmark of Bossey. Adjacent to it, the old building that housed a winepress now serves as the Institute's chapel. For many among the staff and the participants this chapel has become a holy place. Through the decades it was often the heart of life at Bossey, a space for struggles in prayer, silent meditation and corporate worship.

Bossey lies in between two quite different villages. Down below near the lake is *Céligny*, an enclave of the canton of Geneva within the southern part of the canton of Vaud. It is both a wine-growers' village and a place where old Genevese families have stately mansions. On that shore of the lake some famous personalities have lived, like the actor Richard Burton and the pianist Nikita Magaloff, both of whom have given a recital or concert in the Salon blanc. Participants of Bossey meetings know Céligny especially for its church where many of them worship on Sundays, for the small beach where they go swimming on hot summer days, perhaps most for the Café du Soleil, the village pub which serves excellent "fondue" meals.

Towards the Jura lies the Vaudois village of *Bogis-Bossey* whose origins reach back to the early 12th century and to whose municipality the domain of Bossey belongs. Near the road from the château to the village is the Moulin de l'Oie, a watermill dating back to 1610. Bogis-Bossey was originally inhabited only by farmers. Now it has become a place of many villas and flats for people working in Geneva. Together with other villages in the southern part of Vaud this area is called "la terre sainte", the "holy land". The famous abbey of St Maurice owned land in the region from 1150 onwards, and the name comes from those holy brothers, not from any special sanctity of the inhabitants of the region or of Bossey.

The Ecumenical Institute is centrally located, close to three important places: Bonmont, Nyon and Geneva. What remains of the former Cistercian *abbey of Bonmont* stands about seven kilometres to the north, just where the mountain range of the Jura begins to rise. The monks of Bonmont originally owned Bossey. When retracing the history of the château we shall have more information about them.

On the shores of the lake the small town of *Nyon* lies some seven kilometres to the north-east of Bossey: a convenient place for sight-seeing and shopping. History there goes back to the Roman empire; the oldest preserved Roman remains date from the days of Jesus Christ. For persons coming from much later civilizations it is interesting to see these tangible witnesses of New Testament times.

The international city of *Geneva* lies just twenty kilometres south of Bossey. Under its cathedral the remnants of the oldest Christian church in Switzerland have been excavated, dating from just after the middle of the 4th century. Later Geneva became for Europe and beyond the centre of the Calvinist Reformation. Many international organizations are now located in the city, such as the International Labour Office, the International Red Cross, the World Health Organisation, some of the offices of the United Nations Organisation and — for Bossey even more important — the headquarters of several global Christian organizations, including the World Council of Churches (WCC), the world bodies of the YMCA and YWCA, the World Student Christian Federation and two world confessional alliances: the Lutheran World Federation and the World Alliance of Reformed Churches. Both its proximity to such international centres and a certain distance from their bureaucracies were among the reasons for choosing Bossey as the home of the Ecumenical Institute.

An ecumenical conspiracy

More important than a place is the fact that Bossey has become a worldwide fellowship of people from various walks of life, races, cultures and confessions. Most of them had never met or even heard of one another, and members of this strange fellowship can be found today in the most unlikely places. A face may suddenly light up when Bossey is mentioned at a priest's crowded home in an African township of Johannesburg. A similar interest in what the Ecumenical Institute stands for might at times be noticed in a lawyer's office, the home of a business manager or a trade union leader in Western Europe. Bossey may "ring a bell" in such different environments as a church headquarters office in North America, a refugee camp in the Middle East, a women's meeting in Asia, a Vatican office in Rome, an educational colloquium in Latin America, a theological college on a Micronesian atoll in the northern Pacific or a Romanian Orthodox monastery.

Despite diversities of backgrounds and professions there is a *common vision* and a shared commitment which bind many of these people together. In early times this common link was often referred to as an "ecumenical con-spiracy", a fellowship with a common spirit. There certainly are many people who passed through Bossey without coming under its spell, or later abandoned their commitment to the vision they received. Nevertheless, Bossey is not an innocuous or neutral place. People are challenged here to change and deepen their thinking, attitudes and sometimes even their vocations. In the process a few might have lost their faith. Many more have been strengthened in it. A few marriages have broken down in Bossey because one of the couple went through such deep changes that he or she became estranged from the other. More often people have found their life partners at the Institute. Above all, a universal network of lasting friendships has grown in and out of Bossey.

The ecumenical conspiracy works for a conversion, a re-formation in self-sufficient and self-complacent church life. It means an ongoing struggle for a *Christian presence* through common, credible worship, witness and service in the world. There is no fixed curriculum to be followed year after year. Every new group that comes together has its own character, its own specific questions and its own mixture of backgrounds. Ultimately it is not the place, not a given Bossey tradition, and not the resident staff which "make" Bossey what it is. The participants at conferences, courses and in the Graduate School are the main actors. In a real sense "Bossey" has to be reinvented and recreated with each new meeting. New days of confusion, pain and joy must be lived through, new hours of truth experienced.

Various versions of the story

If somehow members of this strange fellowship could be brought together, different memories would come alive. During the last fifty years far-reaching changes have taken place in world history, church history and the ecumenical movement, all of which are reflected in the life and programme of Bossey.

According to their age, people will call to mind different periods in the life of the Institute. Many participants in the early courses are no longer with us. Those whose life journey has not yet ended will remember the days when Hendrik Kraemer and Suzanne de Diétrich formed the leadership team of Bossey in the late 1940s and early 1950s. Others may recall persons and events when, from the mid-1950s to the early 1970s, Hans-Heinrich Wolf and Nikos Nissiotis were directors. The younger people will have memories of the last decades when successively John Mbiti, Karl Hertz, Adriaan Geense, Samuel Amirtham and, since 1990, Jacques Nicole gave direction to life and learning in Bossey.

It is quite likely that the directors and members of the teaching staff might not be among the persons first remembered, but the chauffeur who met participants at Céligny railway station or Geneva airport and the hostess or the receptionist who welcomed them at the château. Many will certainly recall the interpreters, the librarian, the administrative staff, the gardener, the chef and those who keep the house clean. Probably no one would think of Bossey without remembering the "blue angels", young volunteers who since the mid-1950s have come for a few months to help with the household chores of the Institute and who bring to its daily life the charm and freshness of youth. Some of the participants who attended the same conference, course or Graduate School are sure to come alive. Each of these individual recollections could give a special slant to the Bossey story.

A particular group of persons can claim an inside knowledge of what happens at Bossey, the *members of the board*. It has included outstanding lay persons, theologians and church leaders. During their annual meetings, and often in between, they helped the permanent staff to discern priorities, to evaluate critically the work done, and to plan future meetings. They could tell us about the many financial problems, crises in the staff team and all the administrative and pastoral tasks they were called upon to address. Together with the board, the general secretaries of the World Council and a few senior staff members from its headquarters have played an important role in helping to shape and develop the work of the Institute.

Obviously the members of the *permanent staff* will have much to recall. The story would be different if an interpreter, an office secretary or a blue angel were to tell it. This permanent staff is a strange mixture of people, not always easily held together. It does not form a religious community with a common spiritual discipline. Some of them work at Bossey with a deep Christian commitment, others mainly to earn their livelihood or because they like the international setting. There is no common language, although English and French predominate. Some live on the campus, both bachelors and families; others come only for their hours of work. Even among committed Christians in the team it is not possible to have a common eucharistic celebration because there are among them men and women of Orthodox, Roman Catholic and Protestant persuasions. The greatest difficulty for the resident staff is to remain open for the constantly changing composition of the groups. A Bossey meeting can create strong human links within a week or a month, and reach a deep personal level of friendship. One would like to keep contact with at least some of the members of the group that is leaving, but already a new group has arrived.

Special versions of the Bossey story might be told by family members of the resident team. Wives or husbands of teaching staff members without small children to care for have often fully participated in the life and work of the Institute and fulfilled important ministries. Living on the campus with a large family can be quite nerve-racking. Young children of course like Bossey with all the space for playing, all the guests who spoil them and all the room for mischief they can hope for. Rebellious teenagers at times hate this rather isolated place with all the serious adults who talk endlessly. The rhythm of a family with children who go to school often clashes with the daily rhythm of the Institute. The husband or wife on the teaching team is usually near home but never really at home, even during evenings, week-ends and school vacations.

A note on the Bossey experience behind the present version of the story may not be out of place. The author participated in the second youth leaders' course in early 1948, was a student of the third Graduate School (see appendix A) and, as head of the WCC laity department, collaborated a great deal with the staff of the Institute. From 1961 he lived with his family at Bossey for ten years, working as its associate director. Since then he has often returned to the Institute as a resource person. This background marks the general character — and certainly also the bias — of the story as told here. It is told mainly from the point of view of the Institute's programme and the perspective of the teaching staff.

Different agendas

Life and work at Bossey are influenced by different agendas, all of which dictate the priorities. But these agendas do not necessarily coalesce nor do they run parallel to one another. And this creates tensions.

The world's agenda: Setting priorities for the work of the Institute calls for sensitivity to current developments in world history. Programmes must take up the questions and needs of human society so that Christians may be helped to respond to them through prophetic witness and healing service. The experience of life differs from one continent, one social class and one time-span to another, and questions and needs are differently accentuated. For this reason, in spite of the danger of making too sweeping generalizations, each of the following chapters attempts to recall some of the major events and developments that marked the mood and daily life in the period under discussion. Ecumenical history is deeply rooted in human history. What happens in the "oikoumene", the whole inhabited world, is not only the stage or background of the ecumenical movement; it is an integral part of that movement because God works through judgment and grace in the midst of world history. During almost every Bossey meeting a micro-cosmos out of this macro-cosmos is gathered, representing many of the hopes and pains, tensions and struggles of the world.

The agenda of Christian faith: Christian faith brings to the agenda its own points for reflection, prayer and action, providing its specific criteria of judgment. There is one Lord and one faith — but even in this basic affirmation there have been changes in approach and emphasis. In the decades immediately before and after 1946, a strong, unequivocal "biblical theology" informed Christian faith. Then the great diversity of faith testimonies in the Bible was more strongly emphasized. During the early years most participants at the Bossey meetings and the majority of its teaching staff were Protestants from the Western world. Those responsible for the programme had great openness to confessions and cultures other than their own, but a Western and Protestant bias remained. Gradual changes came with increasing Orthodox and Roman Catholic input and through more teachers and participants coming to Bossey from other continents. Moreover, the challenge from faiths other than Christian became stronger. The Bible had to be read also with the eyes of Asians, Africans, Latin Americans and Pacific islanders, from the perspective of the oppressed and the poor, enriched by the experience and insights of women. New accentuations of the common Christian faith had to be discerned through a dialogue of theologies developed in different periods of church history and in different cultures as well as in a dialogue with people of other faiths.

The agenda of the churches: The Ecumenical Institute is part of the World Council of Churches and it must remain sensitive to the life, needs and questions of the churches around the world that have covenanted together to form the Council. The director of Bossey reports to the Council's central committee and it is this committee which, after each assembly, nominates the governing board of the Institute. Whenever the Council restructures its programme, administration and financial policy, this has an impact on Bossey. There is much mutually enriching collaboration between the Institute and various WCC departments and units, but considerable tension and mutual criticism have also come up. The conditions and styles of work in a resident learning community differ from those of a centre of administration with its itinerant staff. Moreover, the questions and needs of the churches around the world are differently perceived when looked at from the point of view of the groups meeting at the Institute and that of WCC headquarters.

The agenda of the staff: Life and work at Bossey have always been strongly influenced by the special gifts, interests and shortcomings of successive directors, and the contributions and failures of the resident teaching and administrative staff. In most periods the main director formed a team with an associate director and one or two short-term assistant directors/lecturers. Differing durations of the period of employment and the specific competences of team members ensured both continuity and the necessary change (see appendix B).

Other factors: The special link of Bossey with the theological faculty of Geneva university has at times influenced decisions concerning the staff and programme of the Institute. In addition Bossey has, like all human institutions, its own internal momentum, uncritically letting traditional work continue and stifling new initiatives. At other times a trendy preference for change implied the risk of giving up valuable traditions. It has been the task of the board of the Institute to maintain the balance between these two tendencies.

Given the diversity of issues discussed and programmes undertaken, it is not possible to make a clear-cut distinction of periods in the history of Bossey, thematic or otherwise. There are gradual changes and overlaps, but the following broad periods may be identified:
— Up to 1946: The origins of the Ecumenical Institute
— 1946-55: The period of the pioneers
— 1955-70: Growing up and reaching out
— 1970-83: Rethinking the role of Bossey
— 1983-96: Looking towards the year 2000

2. The Origins of Bossey

The ecumenical movement did not begin with the World Council of Churches. A long way had already been travelled by Christians and churches together. Those who founded Bossey and the World Council belonged to the second and third ecumenical generations. This story must therefore begin several decades before 1946, the year the Ecumenical Institute was officially opened. Its origins are rooted in the movements which struggled for ecumenical advance before and during the world war. These movements were influenced by world history in the first half of our century and they endeavoured to respond to it.

A world at war

For readers today it is difficult to visualize the world as it was during the early decades of the 20th century. In all continents most people still lived in relatively stable village societies. One could travel by train or ship, but cars and roads for motor traffic were only just being built. Links by telegraph had been established. The telephone was available only in affluent regions, connecting the major cities. Radios were bulky instruments. Travel, postal connections and communication in general were very slow. The majority of the world's inhabitants lived in small communities without much knowledge of the faiths and customs of other communities; they had very little by way of international and intercultural contacts.

Only if we realize this relative isolation of most human communities can we fully appreciate the excitement generated by the *first international meetings*. They were eye-opening events. The need for such encounters across national and religious/ideological frontiers became all the more evident as socio-political developments began to make clear how interdependent human communities are.

Through the *Russian revolution* in 1917 theoretical Marxism became a revolutionary new force in world history. Many saw it as a terrible danger, but the masses of poor and exploited people all over the world perceived it as a new beginning and a sign of hope. Europe had by then lost much of its credibility because of the 1914-18 war. Out of Europe also came, just after that war, the worst epidemic ever experienced, the Spanish 'flu, spreading over half of the globe and killing within a year some twenty million people.

The harshness and injustices of the peace treaty of Versailles led to continuing tensions from Germany to China. The *League of Nations*, created in 1919, had little effective authority. People in Europe were tired and sceptical, forced frequently to live in conditions of famine. North Americans had begun to dream of a new world order based on democracy and economic progress. In colonized countries, and especially in Asia, resistance to both Western imperialism and their own feudal structures grew steadily. Student protests in China began in 1919 and in India the non-violent resistance movement of Mahatma Gandhi slowly gained ground, becoming an inspiration for many around the world.

The dream of a new world based on a capitalist free market system was badly shaken by the Wall Street crash in 1929 which led to a worldwide economic crisis and widespread poverty. This became fertile ground for the spread of *totalitarian ideologies* in Italy, Germany and some Latin American countries. Rooted in different ideologies, totalitarianism also grew in Japan and the Soviet Union. Japan occupied Manchuria and later fought with China; Italy invaded Ethiopia; Germany annexed Austria and parts of Czechoslovakia. The Spanish civil war showed how cruel and pitiless the coming confrontation of ideologies would be.

By September 1939 a *worldwide war* had become inevitable. Japan had already declared a new order for the East and started taking over South-East Asia and the western Pacific. In Europe the German armies marched eastward and then towards the west and south. Seen from a world perspective, different wars were in fact being fought. In Europe it was mainly a struggle between democracy and dictatorship. Outside of Europe it became also a struggle to maintain colonial domination or, for the many Asians and Africans involved, a struggle for freedom, to liberate themselves from Western domination. Oil began to play an important role, which meant that the powerful nations sought to extend their influence in the Middle East. The long years of war ended with the atomic bombs that devastated Hiroshima and Nagasaki in August 1945.

Among peoples and nations *everyday life* was experienced in very different ways. Before the war the majority of the world population simply had to work hard and struggle for survival. In the large rural regions life continued very much as it had been at the beginning of the century. Sports, for instance the Olympic Games, gained an increasing importance in public life. Through a better flow of information the horizon of the more affluent extended to other continents. During the war such places as Dunkirk, Tobruk, Stalingrad, Guadalcanal, Leipzig and later also Dachau and Hiroshima became known all over the world through the widely disseminated news from battlefields and the advancing or retreating fronts.

Despite the differences *basic points of a broad agenda* were becoming urgent for all:

— The monetary crisis and the world war showed that the whole of humanity is interdependent and has a common destiny.

— Many were drawn out of their family circle and social class, because in the emergency of war people of different cultures, races, religions and ideologies had to work and fight together.

— For the first time in history human beings had gained the knowledge and the power to destroy the earth and themselves. The threat of atomic power became part of human destiny.

— The nations made an initial response to such new factors in world history by forming, in June 1945, the United Nations Organisation.

How did Christians and churches respond, and testify to their faith, in this world of war? Let us look at the *vision and work of five pioneers* who were the fathers and mothers of the Ecumenical Institute.

Keller's dream

The first to envisage something like the later Ecumenical Institute was the Swiss Reformed theologian Adolf Keller. He had worked in Cairo as a young pastor and, with his knowledge of Arabic, had begun to establish links with the Islamic world and with Orthodox churches. After the 1914-18 war he visited the USA, and he returned to Europe with plans to work on a number of ecumenical projects. As secretary of the Swiss Federation of Protestant Churches he became in 1922 the main initiator and director of the European Central Office for Inter-Church Aid. Through that office both American and European churches responded to the suffering and need in Europe, helping Protestants and Orthodox from Spain to Russia. Material aid was linked to a programme of scholarships and leadership training. One of the donors for this work was John D. Rockefeller Jr, who later also provided the money for starting the Bossey Institute.

Keller soon discovered that *the churches were ill prepared* for being present as agents of prophetic witness and priestly reconciliation in a world of war. Ecumenical youth movements had already done much pioneering work. Among missionaries in the non-Western world some awareness of the changing world situation was growing. In the International Missionary Council, constituted in 1921, a few voices from Asian and African Christians could be heard, but the urgency of their appeals was seldom appreciated. The official churches still hardly knew one another. Ignorance led to mutual suspicion, in turn leading to prejudices and labels. With a few significant exceptions Roman Catholics still stayed out of any corporate study and action with other churches. Among Orthodox and Protestant church leaders the conviction grew that in order to respond both to the demands of the gospel and to the world's agenda Christians had to meet and work together. This led to the creation of two official ecumenical agencies: the movement for Life and Work with its constituting first world conference at Stockholm in 1925, and the movement for Faith and Order with its first world conference at Lausanne in 1927.

From the start Keller was involved in the preparatory work for the *Stockholm conference*. The message of that gathering called on the churches to apply the gospel "in all realms of human life — industrial, social, political and international". But what did the "gospel" mean? When Protestants or Orthodox Christians coming from North America or from Europe prayed that God's kingdom may come, what did they hope for? The uncertainty that marked the world situation also affected the beliefs and conduct of Christians. An intensive theological search began, first in the Faith and Order movement, but soon also in the movement for Life and Work.

Keller was asked to plan and direct the International Christian Social Institute, set up in Geneva to work alongside the International Labour Office. As a professor at Geneva university he created a new theological discipline, that of comparing and studying *the churches' self-understanding* (comparative ecclesiology). Through publications and guest lectures, given at major theological schools in North America and Europe, he interpreted the churches to one another. Already in 1925 he had published the very first book in English on the European crisis theology which was then just developing on the basis of new biblical thinking and in response to growing totalitarianism. He was also the person who brought together for the first time Orthodox and Protestant theological teachers in Eastern Europe.

In the course of this work Keller became convinced that books, lectures and short-term conferences were not enough for serious ecumenical studies. Leading thinkers and students from different confessions and continents had to be brought together into a resident community of learning. He therefore proposed in 1928 that a permanent teaching centre should be established, a "graduate school of ecumenical studies". For this project he won the support of both the theological faculty of Geneva university and the movement for Life and Work. It was planned to start in 1932, but because of the world economic crisis for the time being only ecumenical summer schools, the international theological seminars, could be organized.

The first of these three-week *Geneva seminars* was held in 1934. It was conducted simultaneously in three languages on a budget of just 3500 Swiss francs, partly paid out of Keller's own pocket. The 35 participants, all mature students and young theologians, came from West and East Europe, Great Britain and North America. They stayed in the YMCA hostel and the university provided class-rooms and other facilities. Among the teachers were Emil Brunner from Zurich, F.L. Cross from Oxford, Martin Dibelius from Heidelberg, D. Homrighausen from Indianapolis and J. Cassian from the Russian Orthodox academy in Paris. The programme was made up of lectures, seminars and visits to international institutions in Geneva. The person responsible for practical arrangements and interpretation was well known to many participants at early Bossey meetings: Arnold Mobbs, who later became the pastor of Céligny. A life-long friend of the Ecumenical Institute, he later wrote an account of its early years.

In his report on this first Geneva seminar, Keller once again brought up his proposal for a longer-term *residential graduate school*. He suggested a relationship between this school and Geneva university very similar to the one established twenty years later between Bossey and the Geneva theological faculty. His proposals also included the project for organizing extension work through short-term seminars in the USA and the Orthodox world. By 1935 plans for establishing the permanent set-up were well advanced, and Karl Barth from Bonn had been asked to become a resident lecturer.

Again world events came in the way. The *three-week summer schools* were nevertheless continued, maintaining a high academic standard. Participants numbered up to a hundred, not counting the auditors and audiences at the large public sessions. Among the teachers were Karl Barth, Jaques Courvoisier (later moderator of the board of the Bossey Graduate School), Walter Horton, Reinhold Niebuhr, Paul Tillich, Stefan Zankov and Willem A. Visser 't Hooft. For one of the seminars Toyohiko Kagawa from Japan was persuaded to offer a course on Christian social ethics. The themes of these schools covered a wide range: biblical and dogmatic reflections on the kingdom of God, issues of social ethics, the history of the ecumenical movement and comparative ecclesiology.

These seminars marked only a partial realization of Keller's dream, but were nevertheless worthy predecessors of the Graduate School of Ecumenical Studies which started at Bossey in 1952. Some of Keller's experiences and conclusions are still valid:

> Experience has shown that the present organization of the programme including central biblical and systematic subjects as well as the theological questions of the ecumenical movement and problems of modern church history is entirely justified.
>
> It seems desirable that the members of the seminar should live together in the same house during the whole time of the seminar, in spite of advantages that a town like Geneva offers. It is therefore contemplated to convene future seminars in places outside of the town where all could live together.

Oldham's vision of the churches' vocation

Keller anticipated the later theological encounters and confessional studies at Bossey, but it was Joseph H. Oldham who pioneered what became in Bossey's early period the central issues: church-world relationships and the role of the laity. Both the early movements of Life and Work and Faith and Order appeared like an army of officers without troops. Church leaders and theologians were present, but the large majority of Christians involved in secular professions and attempting to be present as Christ's witnesses in the structures of society were hardly represented. The Geneva seminars had served the officers and not the laity. Another serious limitation of the two movements was their preoccupation with questions raised in the societies and the divided churches of Europe and North America. The "East" meant for them mainly Russia or the Orthodox churches, the "West" pointed to Western Europe and North America or to the Protestants and Roman Catholics in these regions. The issues raised in Asia, Africa and Latin America were rarely discussed.

For thinking in terms of the whole of church membership and the whole world Oldham's work became crucial. Oldham was born in Bombay in an officer's family, of Scottish descent. There he spent his early childhood, playing with Indian children. He studied in Edinburgh and Oxford with the aim of entering the civil service in India. A strong commitment to Christ led him also to study theology, but not with a view to working as a priest. He served the church and the world as an Anglican layman. Oldham had the great gift of discerning the need of the hour in a changing world situation and concentrating on this one issue. He did so with stubbornness until he achieved what he wanted. Only then would he turn his attention to another focus of obedience. The title of one of his early books indicates programmatically the twin agendas of his life-long work: *The World and the Gospel*. By confronting the demands and promises of the gospel with the specific needs and hopes of the world (of Asia and Africa as well as of Europe and the Americas), Oldham gained a new vision of the churches' vocation.

First he concentrated on Christian student work in Great Britain and India. Then John R. Mott got him to organize the major world mission conference in 1910 at Edinburgh. Already evident there was *Oldham's method* of ecumenical study and action. Organizing meant for him both careful administration and rigorous intellectual preparatory work. He sought and gathered creative thinkers for the issue in focus, among them outstanding decision-makers in the secular world. Proceeding in the Socratic way of asking questions, he stimulated corporate thinking, leading to new and relevant actions. In ecumenical history, perhaps no conferences and consultations have been prepared with such thoroughness as those for which Oldham was responsible. His ways and standards of work later became the model for those who organized frontier conferences at Bossey, though they seldom reached his high level of excellence.

The following are three of the *life and death issues* to which Oldham turned his attention and which became also central in the work of Bossey.

• Racism: An enquiry, conducted mainly in Africa, produced influential publications on the churches' task with regard to race and education. It also led to the creation of the International Institute of African Languages and Cultures and helped to change British colonial policy in Kenya.

• Secularism: In this understanding of life which dogmatically asserts that the whole of reality is confined to this time and earth, Oldham saw *the* adversary with which Christian faith is confronted in all continents, particularly in what was then still called the "Christian" West. He persuaded the International Missionary Council to make secularism a major subject of its world conference at Jerusalem in 1928.

• Church, Community and State: Under Oldham's leadership this became the theme of the second world conference of Life and Work in Oxford in 1937. Crucial agenda points of the pre-war world situation were taken up: What should be the response to emerging totalitarian states? What kind of education fosters a truly human life in community? How can churches be present as heralds of and forces for God's kingdom in human history?

It was in connection with this last question about the church and its function in society that Oldham stated his basic convictions on *the role of the laity*. In the preparatory study for Oxford he made the distinction between the church as an assembly for worship, teaching and corporate service and the church as it exists from day to day through the life Christians live in the world. He pointed to the great gap between the concerns normally discussed in the assembled church and the reality experienced by lay people in their world of daily work.

> If the Christian faith is to bring about changes in the present and the future, as it has done in the past, in the thought, habits and practices of society, it can only do this through being a living, working faith of the multitudes of laymen and women involved in the ordinary affairs of life. The only way in which it can affect business or politics is by shaping the convictions and determining the actions of those engaged in business and politics... We stand before a great historic task — the task of restoring the lost unity between worship and work.

This was of course not a totally new insight. But Oldham persistently prodded church leaders and theologians to go beyond talking about the role of the laity, and to explore what it means for the understanding of Christ's church, its worship, teaching and mission.

The war broke out. Christians in many walks of life now painfully discovered the *gap between church life and society* about which Oldham had written. As soldiers at the front, as prisoners of war or inmates of concentration camps they met committed secular humanists, Marxists and believers of other living faiths. They realized how ill equipped they were to be credible witnesses. It was important to have places where people from different walks of life could meet for seeking together God's purpose and direction. In Scotland a group of laymen and ministers had formed the Iona community, linking worship and work within a daily discipline, thus helping its members to be the church in and for industrial society. In the Christian Frontier Council Oldham himself brought together a small but influential group of British lay people in civil service, business and other professions for discovering the implications of the Christian faith for the affairs of the nation.

Around 1945 several *fellowships and centres for lay training* were started, almost at the same time, in many countries: the Protestant Professional Associations in France, the Kerk en Wereld (Church and World) institute in Holland, the Evangelical Academy at Bad Boll in Germany, the Agape centre in Italy. Later similar initiatives developed in North America, such as the Parishfield centre near Detroit, and in Asia and Africa, like the Christian academies in Japan and Korea and the Mindolo centre in Zambia. The same vision of Christian presence in the world through the ministry of the laity inspired other new beginnings: industrial missions, the German Kirchentag, religious brotherhoods and sisterhoods open to the world. The Ecumenical Institute at Bossey became part of this worldwide movement and was soon asked to function as its rallying point.

Visser 't Hooft's contribution

The one who, even more than Keller and Oldham, became the father of Bossey was Willem A. Visser 't Hooft, a man with broad interests and a sense of strategy. Keller asked this young Dutchman to add a world perspective to the Geneva seminars. Oldham had the backing of most church leaders when in 1937 he convinced Visser 't

Hooft, then the general secretary of the World Student Christian Federation, to accept the call to become the secretary of the proposed World Council of Churches.

Visser 't Hooft described himself as a generalist, one who knows less and less about more and more. He described his writings as "interpretations across confessional and linguistic frontiers of thoughts which I have picked up from the theological path-finders" — an apt description of what later members of the teaching staff at Bossey were called to become. The path-finders who met in Visser 't Hooft's home or in meetings he convened were a remarkable group: Protestant, Orthodox and Roman Catholic theologians and philosophers like Karl Barth, Reinhold Niebuhr, Nicolas Berdyaev, Stefan Zankov and Yves Congar, including quite early representatives from churches in Asia such as Sarah Chakko and D.T. Niles. He was also in constant contact with the ecclesiastical path-finders of the early ecumenical movement, the leaders of Life and Work and Faith and Order. During the war Visser 't Hooft's Geneva home sometimes also became the secret meeting place for members of resistance movements against Nazism, among them Dietrich Bonhoeffer. By such gatherings of various path-finders he drew together divergent strands of the ecumenical move-ment. He brought together the concerns of both Keller and Oldham and helped to interlink the ecumenical youth movements with the more official ecumenical organizations. Later he transmitted this concern for the wholeness of the ecumenical movement to the leaders of Bossey.

A *God-centred reading of the Bible* informed Visser 't Hooft's thinking and action. What he wrote in the 1930s about the role of the Bible became guiding convictions for many of those who worked to establish the World Council. These convictions also marked the early period of the Ecumenical Institute: "The Bible once more becomes our meeting place. As Christians, coming from different directions, we will meet here — or nowhere. The future of our unity depends on our willingness to make this pilgrimage together." "The Bible becomes silent when we try to force it to answer our questions. It speaks when we come to it as seekers for the truth of God. The alternative is not whether we read the Bible 'piously' or 'critically', but whether we read it egocentrically or theocentrically."

Even before the war ended, in May 1945, Visser 't Hooft and two other European ecumenical spokesmen flew to New York to hold consultations with American church leaders. The team informed the Americans about the spiritual and political realities of the European situation so that they could corporately plan the work of reconstruction. At a private dinner the visitors were asked to speak about the life of the churches in Europe during the war. Among the dinner guests was a multi-millionaire, a Baptist layman who, before the war, had helped European churches. He asked Visser 't Hooft to meet him the following day.

The visit, in the top office of the Rockefeller centre, proved to be of crucial importance for Bossey. *John D. Rockefeller, Jr*, wanted to know what the projected World Council of Churches planned to do in responding to the post-war situation. "I had to do some quick thinking," recalls Visser 't Hooft:

> We had many plans, and the great question was which would be of greatest interest to Mr Rockefeller. But it soon became clear that he was especially interested in the plan to create an ecumenical institute which would confront young people who had to rebuild their lives after the years in the armies or in resistance movements with the challenge of renewal in the life of the churches and the nations.

Visser 't Hooft must indeed have done some very quick thinking based on a sudden inspiration. The minutes of the Provisional Committee for the World Council up to May 1945 give no indication that such an institute had actually been planned. Once, in late 1944 the committee discussed a proposal that an American be appointed for doing "ecumenical education" in Europe. Visser 't Hooft then suggested tentatively that such work might also involve "running an ecumenical centre somewhere in Switzerland". Keller's dream had apparently not been totally forgotten. However, no action was taken on this matter.

Rockefeller was pleased with the more detailed memorandum which Visser 't Hooft later submitted. He only commented that for the anticipated budget more money ought to have been asked. After a few months a cheque for one million dollars was received, with the suggestion that half of it might be used for the work of reconstruction of church life in Europe and the other half for establishing an ecumenical institute. Thanks to this generous grant, almost two years before the World Council was finally inaugurated, the Ecumenical Institute could start its work of training and study. Rockefeller obviously felt that the money had been well spent; contrary to his normal policy, he twice more helped Bossey financially.

The result of another of Visser 't Hooft's initiatives, the *Stuttgart declaration*, strongly influenced the work of the Ecumenical Institute in its early years. The question of war guilt had surfaced again. In 1918 it had been a delicate and divisive issue. In October 1945 Visser 't Hooft went with an ecumenical delegation to meet with German church leaders at Stuttgart for re-establishing fraternal contacts, and to have a frank conversation with them. This meeting led to a courageous and widely publicized declaration by the Council of the German Evangelical Church. The great suffering brought to many people and nations by Nazi Germany was publicly acknowledged. Among the signatories many had been in the forefront of the spiritual struggle against the National Socialist regime. Yet they stated: "We accuse ourselves for not witnessing more courageously, for not praying more faithfully, for not believing more joyously and for not loving more ardently. Now a new beginning is to be made in our churches." This declaration opened the way for German churches to become founding members of the World Council. From the very first courses and conferences, the Germans participated fully in the work of the Bossey Institute.

Suzanne's friendship

The person who brought to Bossey the rich experience of ecumenical youth movements, especially of the World Student Christian Federation, was *Suzanne de Diétrich*. One student generation after another, and from 1946 onwards the many participants of Bossey meetings as well, simply called her "Suzanne", with affection and respect. We shall follow their example.

Suzanne's life journey was an unusual one. She was born into a rich, noble family in northern Alsace, owners of a large industrial enterprise. The de Dietrich factories needed engineers, and Suzanne became one of the first women engineers in the French-speaking world. Although she never practised that profession she continued to look at the world around her with the seriousness and precision of an engineer's eyes. During her student days she had come into contact with Christian youth work. She took up full-time work, first for the French Student Christian Movement in Paris and then with the World's Student Christian Federation in Geneva. Despite a congenital infirmity she had travelled widely in Europe, North America, the Indian sub-continent and Latin America before starting work at Bossey.

A certain *earthly spirituality* marked Suzanne's whole personality and work. She was passionately present on this earth and at the same time she appeared to inhabit a world and time beyond our own. With a holy horror of intellectual dishonesty and hypocritical piety, she held together a deep involvement in this world's struggles and a perspective of eternity. Her life thus seemed to have a prophetic and transcendent quality. The prophets of the Bible were her special friends. In 1938 she triggered a heated public discussion through her prophetic protest against her country's yielding to Hitler's pressure in the Munich agreements. A year later she helped to set up the CIMADE, a French ecumenical aid agency deeply involved in politics. Such socio-political action was rooted in Bible study and prayer. For years she meditated upon John's gospel. In 1932 she helped to organize what must have been the first residential, fully ecumenical retreat, gathering outstanding Orthodox, Roman Catholic and Protestant thinkers from different countries for corporate study and prayer.

Impressed by her rich experience and world perspective Visser 't Hooft recruited Suzanne for Bossey. She herself had other plans. After many years of international work her wish was to return to France and to become involved more concretely at *the frontier between the church and the world*. Towards the end of the war the movement of the Protestant professional associations had been created, groups of businessmen, medical doctors, educators and social workers meeting to explore what it meant to be Christians in their professions. Suzanne had been asked to become the coordinator of these associations. Now she was called to do a very similar work on a world level.

Suzanne liked to quote J.R. Mott's saying that the World Student Christian Federation is a *movement of friendships*. In more official ecumenical organizations questions of delegated church representation, agreed statements and deep respect for ecclesiastical authorities had to be given due weight. It was therefore important that the ecumenical movement continue to develop also with freedom and spontaneity, so that daring experiments could be tried. Suzanne brought the understanding of the ecumenical movement as a movement of friendships to bear on the life and work of Bossey. What she had learned in the World Student Christian Federation stood her in good stead at the Institute. Bossey was to create another universal network of friendships, making up for the growing tendency towards ecumenical institutionalization and bureaucratic delays.

Friendships in student work developed through *corporate Bible study*. At the end of the 19th century such study was pursued mainly through daily devotional reading of the Bible, called the "morning watch", and by inspiring evangelistic talks typical of the great revival movements. By the turn of the 20th century, partly through the wide use of a Bible study book by Oldham, an intellectually more demanding kind of group study developed in the British Student Christian Movement. From the 1920s onwards Suzanne popularized this type of Bible study in all continents through her leadership, travels and writings. The insights of biblical scholarship and the critical questions and doubts of students with regard to the Bible were taken seriously, and the Bible itself now addressed inescapable questions to the students. Such study was undertaken not only to promote personal spiritual nurture but also to help confront the prevalent ideologies and to equip people for corporate witness and service in the socio-political world. This way of holding together the Bible's agenda and the world's agenda later marked much of the life and work at Bossey.

From the early days *friendship links across cultural and socio-political frontiers* developed in Christian student work. Even in the early decades of this century student movements in Europe, Britain, North America, China, Japan, India and South Africa fully participated in the World Federation. Since 1908 *The Student World* — the first ecumenical journal — maintained contacts within the wide range of its membership. With growing political tensions during the 1914-18 war and the uncertainty of the following decades it was difficult to maintain the fellowship. At the Federation's general committee meeting in Peking in 1922 questions of war and peace and of racial relations deeply divided the student delegates. A minority felt that they would have to sacrifice what they believed as the truth for the sake of unity. The Federation had to learn to stay together while disagreeing and corporately to seek the truth within and beyond the partial understandings of it. Suzanne would later have to help many groups at Bossey to maintain the same kind of fellowship despite socio-political and cultural divisions.

Friendship across confessional frontiers is by no means less costly. As early as in 1911 the Federation leaders visited Orthodox students in Russia and convened the general committee meeting near Constantinople with the blessing of the Ecumenical Patriarch. After the Russian revolution the leaders of the Russian student movement in exile played a prominent part in Federation work, among them Nicolas Berdyaev, Leon Zander and Paul Evdokimov. This meant that prevalent Protestant attitudes, spiritualities and ways of Bible study were being questioned and that the reality and challenge of different confessional traditions had to be taken much more seriously. Suzanne experienced this in 1930 when she was asked to lead a training course in Poland with Orthodox, Roman Catholic and Protestant student leaders of East Europe:

> Humanly speaking, there was no ground for meeting, in temperament, strong national feelings, ecclesiastical membership, and theological conceptions. There were crises. There always are if you go beyond superficial friendships, and if ecumenical dialogue is taken seriously. We make one another suffer, because the truth of God is at stake which each one comprehends from a different point of view.

At Bossey many such crises would occur and Suzanne would have to help groups to transform them into growing experiences.

The greatest contribution of ecumenical student work to Bossey was undoubtedly the large number of *ecumenically trained leaders*. During the early years of the Institute all of the resident staff as well as most board members and speakers had received their ecumenical education in the student movement. Even before the Ecumenical Institute was officially opened the general committee of the Federation had met in the summer of 1946 at the Château de Bossey, and one of its decisions was "that Suzanne remain on the staff until the end of 1946, but on loan to the Ecumenical Institute from 1 October onwards".

Kraemer's vision

The first director of Bossey, Hendrik Kraemer, brought to his leadership and teaching at the Ecumenical Institute remarkable resources of knowledge and experience. Suzanne wrote:

> Kraemer is ecumenical in the most literal sense of the term, for the whole world is "his home"... The universality of his knowledge has something

almost overwhelming for his fellow workers. He always seems to have read everything important, be it in theology, philosophy, sociology, missiology, psychology, history and even in literature. It is this passionate interest in all human thought worth of the name which enables him to engage in true dialogue with the world. He knows that all authentic communication between human beings requires a double intelligence, that of the head and that of the heart. He knows how to read, but also how to listen.

It has been said that Kraemer's head was not simply modelled by God but chiselled out of granite. His youth and apprenticeship were hard, making him a self-made man and a fighter. The son of poor immigrant parents from Germany who lived in Amsterdam, Kraemer early became an orphan. First he was with a militant socialist family and then in a narrowly religious Reformed orphanage. He began to read the Bible on his own as a young teenager, and declared that he would either become a militant socialist or a Christian missionary. He became both. He was accepted in a new mission school, but in the final exams he failed in dogmatics, and he was never ordained. Early in life his gift for languages was discovered. When in 1907 Oldham visited the Netherlands Kraemer served as his interpreter and the two became friends. Without ever going through the high school, Kraemer started university studies in Arabic, Asian languages and Indonesian Islam, while serving as president of the Dutch Student Christian Movement.

Through continuing Bible study and his wide range of readings and encounters Kraemer developed his vision of world history and of the churches' vocation. Later he called it *biblical realism*. The Bible, he wrote,

> is a book of infinite spiritual discovery... This intense realism of the Bible proclaims and asserts realities. It does not intend to present a "world view", but it challenges man in his total being to confront himself with these realities and accordingly take decisions... Pascal, that acute and great mind, discovered the revolutionary and revealing character of this biblical realism in the night of his conversion. He wrote down that night the famous affirmation: "Dieu! Dieu d'Abraham, d'Isaac et de Jacob! Dieu de Jésus Christ, non des philosophes ou des savants", and Pascal knew what he was talking about, as he is admittedly known as one of the most brilliant philosophical and scholarly minds that have ever appeared in human history. It could not be better expressed that the essential message and content of the Bible is always the living, eternally active God, the indubitable Reality, from whom, by whom and for whom all things are.

Obedience to this vision led Kraemer to work for fifteen years as a consultant for the Dutch Bible Society in Indonesia (then the Dutch Indies). There he befriended Indonesian intellectuals of the growing nationalist movement. On the basis of these contacts he helped both Western missionaries and Indonesian Christians to prepare for the coming Asian revolution. Through his travels, publications and vigorous participation in the world missionary conferences at Jerusalem (1928) and Tambaram (1938) he became a well-known figure. Returning to the Netherlands before the war he immediately became involved in a growing church renewal movement.

In 1942 Kraemer was arrested and sent to the hostage camp of St Michielsgestel in the south-western province of Brabant in the Netherlands. He had joined the struggle against the Nazi ideology. At that time professor of history and phenomenology of religion at Leiden university, Kraemer had, along with others, protested against the dismissal of Jewish professors. The German occupying power hoped to break such spiritual and intellectual resistance by imprisoning its leaders and using them as hostages. Life at St Michielsgestel, the confiscated campus of a Roman Catholic seminary, was not as harsh as in the concentration camps. Yet, in retaliation against alleged acts of sabotage, groups of hostages were arbitrarily picked out and shot without trial. Living under the constant threat of death, one inevitably reflects on the ultimate purpose of life.

The hostages, prominent in politics, economics and church life and various university disciplines, secretly created a university in the camp. Instead of breaking their opposition the occupying power had in fact provided them an opportunity for corporate thinking and planning about resistance and the nation's future. Christians, secular humanists and Marxists taught one another and learned together. Kraemer shared with fellow hostages his insights on Asian nationalism and Islam. With his thirst for new learning he keenly followed their teaching in many fields of knowledge. Suffering since youth from insomnia, he now taught himself, during the long nights at the camp, still another Asian language, Tamil, whose rich literature he wanted to read.

Long before interdisciplinary work started at Bossey the future director of the Ecumenical Institute was thus involved in similar work. More than ever he became convinced of the need to *relate church life and the world's burning questions*. Like Oldham he observed that what academic theologians and church synods discussed had little to do with Christian life and witness in the secular world. Together with other Christian leaders detained at St Michielsgestel, Kraemer planned a campaign for building up living local congregations which would be firmly grounded in biblical knowledge and open to the questions of the world. Lay people would have to play an important role, and the training of pastors would have to be directed towards helping church members to be present as Christians in their professional life, in public affairs and families. The plans included also the creation of a national centre; and Kerk en Wereld was in fact inaugurated in autumn 1945 at Driebergen.

Earlier in that same year Kraemer had been a member of the ecumenical team which went to Stuttgart for *meeting with the German church leaders*. Visser 't Hooft recalls how, after the statements of two German spokesmen,

> the first to answer on the WCC side was Dr Kraemer of Holland. He said that there was no hatred in the hearts of the Christians in Holland. Those who had suffered much had learned to be merciful in their judgment. He hoped we could all speak together as standing before God. He had heard with deep emotion what Pastor Asmussen and Pastor Niemöller had said. He understood this as a call to his own church also, that it could only live by the forgiveness of sins. It could not be a matter of bartering. In the light of what had been said the other churches could now say to the German church that they were also ready to accept their responsibility for what happened in Germany.

No wonder that during its first post-war meeting the Provisional Committee of the World Council of Churches (in process of formation) decided in February 1946 to call on this man for directing its Ecumenical Institute.

To be obedient to the vision received was Kraemer's persistent concern. And this vision he passed on to participants of successive meetings at Bossey. One of his last meditations in the chapel of the Institute was based on Paul's defence before king Agrippa in Caesarea (Acts 26): "I was not disobedient to the heavenly vision!"

Bonmont and Bossey

Now that funds for establishing the Ecumenical Institute had been secured, the search for a place began. On a rainy day in the winter of 1945-46 Visser 't Hooft and Robert C. Mackie, the future moderator of the executive board of the Institute, made an exploratory trip in the Geneva region. They had already visited several places which could become the home of the planned Institute, but they were not satisfied. Now they stood in the freezing salons of the Château de Bossey.

No doubt the domain would look beautiful on a sunny day with its grand view, its majestic trees, what remained of the medieval buildings and the present mansion. But on that foggy afternoon it was less than welcoming. During the war it had been used for Polish officers who, after fighting with the allied forces, had sought refuge in Switzerland when the German armies over-ran France. Now the house was empty, run down and uncared-for. With its parquet floors and odd mixture of 18th-century and modern furniture, it seemed ill equipped to become a training centre for young people. Moreover, wherever one turned, one was confronted by Napoleon. The father of the last owner, Colonel Chenevière, had been a great admirer of the French emperor, a passion not likely to be shared by young people from various nations who had been in recent years victims of too many military strategies and battles!

The historian Guillaume Fatio had told the two visitors about the interesting past of the place. The first written source mentioning the medieval domain of Bossey indicates that in 1125 the bishop of Geneva, Humbert de Grammont, donated this property to the Abbey of Bonmont (Bon-mont, the "good mountain"). Like the village Bogis-Bossey and other rural settlements at the foot of the Jura, the domain of Bossey was also for three centuries a "grange", a rural outpost of Bonmont. Cistercian lay brothers lived there to work in the vineyards and fields, joined during the day time by a few monks. Both Visser 't Hooft and Mackie had a keen sense of history. They must have been interested to hear that Bossey once had a chapel. They also heard about what happened to the domain during the Reformation, about the colourful succession of owners since then, and the role Bossey had played in the ecclesiastical and cultural history of the region. This impressed them and they tried to imagine how Bossey would look on a bright summer day. It was sufficiently far from Geneva, but close enough to the headquarters of the proposed World Council. This is the place, they decided. However, because the whole future of the Institute was still rather uncertain, they decided that the château should not be bought straightaway, but only rented for five years.

An extant document reports on *the foundation of the abbey of Bonmont*. The lord of Divonne (a place near Bossey, at the foot of the French Jura) had died. In his memory his wife Helvide and their two sons Walcherius and Stephanus decided to found a place of prayer in their region. They called on the Benedictines of Balerne (a monastery in the French Jura no longer in existence) to send some monks to settle near the present village of Chéserex on forest land which in 1123 they donated for this purpose. Moses, the first abbot and leader of the group of some twelve monks who came, was an acquaintance of Bernard de Clairvaux. Initially the brothers lived apart, like eastern hermits, clearing the forest for cultivation and meeting only for common prayer in a simple wooden chapel. Later they opted for a more ordered community life, and asked to be accepted into the Cistercian renewal movement. In 1131 Bonmont became the first Cistercian monastery in Switzerland, linked with Clairvaux as its mother abbey.

With its particular *Cistercian spirituality* Bonmont developed rapidly. The abbey church, Notre Dame de Bonmont, which still stands, was built before 1150. Excavations have unearthed the foundations and remnants of a cloister, a refectory and a dormitory, a hospital, a house for lay brothers, and surrounding rural buildings. The monks now lived together, keeping strictly St Benedict's monastic rule with its emphasis on a life of prayer and manual labour. The white/grey-clad brothers daily spent six hours in prayer, starting at 2 in the morning. According to the seasons several hours were set apart for manual work and two to five hours for reading. As donations came in, more and more land was brought under cultivation. Eventually the monks must have been outnumbered by the lay brothers who spent more hours in manual work.

The Cistercians of Bonmont became influential. In Geneva they had a house for selling wine and, close to Geneva, a mill. Some eighty villages and domains are mentioned as belonging to the abbey. Such extensive land ownership became one of the reasons for the decline of Bonmont. With fewer lay brothers, workers for the harvests had to be hired, and the peasants began to revolt. The monastic discipline declined. Even before the abbey was secularized at the time of the Reformation it had lost much of its spiritual and secular influence. The Protestant Bernese conquered the region of Vaud in 1536. They invited Nikolaus Zurkinden, a Reformed theologian, to become governor of the bailiwick of Bonmont to which Bossey then belonged. With the stones of the decaying monastery a manor house was built. When, in the revolutionary movements of 1798, the Bernese rule ended and the region of Vaud became part of the Lemanic Republic, the remaining possessions of the bailiwick of Bonmont were sold. The Bernese had used the church of Bonmont as a cheese dairy. It subsequently became a wine cellar and a barn. In 1942 Notre Dame de Bonmont was classified as a historical monument and, more recently, restored. It is a sign of the times that the domain of Bonmont has now become a country club with a golf course.

A different development marked the history of Bossey. An inventory of 1485 indicates that the domain consisted of the tower and the winepress, some other buildings which have since disappeared, and about 30 acres of vineyards, 20 acres of arable land and several pastures. In 1536 this domain was sold to Antoine Saunier, a French refugee from the Dauphiné who became the Reformed preacher at Perroy and Rolle and later director of the recently established Protestant college in Lausanne. Saunier had collaborated much with one of the main reformers of French-speaking Switzerland, Guillaume Farel, the man who convinced Calvin that he should stay in Geneva. When Calvin heard that Saunier had acquired the former church property of Bossey he severely reprimanded him.

Saunier's son sold the domain, and subsequently there were several lords of Bossey. The family which owned the place longest was the Turretinis, starting with Jean Turretini, an Italian Protestant refugee who had become a rich businessman in Geneva. He lost his wealth when one of his more ambitious projects failed — the attempt to link the lakes of Geneva and Neuchâtel by a canal. After several other owners the domain came back to the Turretini family. Around 1720 the present château was built by Horace-Benedict Turretini. After the abolition of the feudal system in 1798 the domain passed from one private owner to another.

The most famous among them was a French Protestant writer, *Baroness Germaine de Staël-Necker*. Influenced by Rousseau she had gathered the intellectual revolutionaries in her "salon" of Paris. In 1803 she was banished from France and during her exile the château of Coppet not far from Bossey became her home. There, in between her European travels, she actively participated in discussions with many European intellectuals and artists whom she invited to her home. She bought the Château de Bossey in 1809 to put up her guests. It was also to serve as the home of her son Auguste who, however, sold it a couple of years later.

A true château must have a ghost. Elisabeth Lange, another owner, is linked with *Bossey's ghost story*. She was a beautiful actress from Paris, married to Jean Simons, a rich Belgian businessman and ship-owner who bought the château for her in 1817. "La bonne châtelaine de Bossey", as the actress was called, died in 1825 when she was on a cure in Italy. Her husband could not reconcile himself to living without his beautiful wife, and he had her body embalmed and brought it back to Bossey in a coffin with a crystal cover. For almost a year he kept her in the Salon blanc. When the police ordered him to bury the body he promised to do so in the park of Bossey. However, around midnight he secretly took the body to the Catholic church in Carouge just outside Geneva. There ends the story. But the tomb of the "bonne châtelaine" has never been found and it is said that since then strange things have happened and strange noises have been heard on the second floor of the château.

Among the *19th-century owners of Bossey* were two artists: Firmin Massot, Germaine de Staël's favourite painter, and Massot's most talented pupil, Amélie Munier-Romilly, a well-known portrait painter married to a Genevese pastor and professor of Hebrew. Later the ownership of the château passed on to a Scot and then to a French count who kept his collection of Italian paintings in the Orangerie.

The last private owner of Bossey was the Chenevière family. Alice Chenevière bought it in 1904. Her husband collected all the portraits, battle scenes and caricatures of Napoleon he could get, which participants of the early Bossey courses may still remember. Their son, Fernand Chenevière, lived in the near-by mansion and farm, "Petite-Coudre", and leased the château as a holiday home for European aristocrats. From 1930 to 1939 Bossey was rented out by the famous American Smith College for women. The students came for a year's stay to study European culture and get acquainted with the work of the League of Nations in Geneva. So there were balls and concerts in the château long before students from all over the world began celebrating their cultural evenings during the semesters of the Graduate School of Ecumenical Studies.

3. The Period of the Pioneers: 1946-1955

5 October 1946: the Ecumenical Institute was officially opened at the Château de Bossey. The inaugural lecture was given by its director, Hendrik Kraemer, on "The Christian Church in a World of Crisis". Kraemer did not attempt a socio-political analysis of the critical world situation but rather showed how, behind this situation, lay a spiritual crisis.

Trusting in the power of human self-determination, of science and technology, said Kraemer, the masses of people in all continents believed that they could become fully in charge of their life, of their individual and corporate destiny. Yet in this search for progress the very basis of all great civilizations, the sense of transcendence, was gradually being lost. The process of secularization led not only to the liberations that were needed but also to "a self-created emptiness" which in turn increased disorientation and a fear of life. In this crisis of the world, which also affected Christians, the churches needed to rediscover and reaffirm the cosmic dimension of salvation as expressed in Paul's letter to the Ephesians. The world must be seen where in fact it is, at the foot of the cross from which Christ reigns. The orb and the cross: to see these together was the vocation of Bossey.

The post-war world

Paradoxically, in the year the United Nations was founded, *this orb was divided into two*: in the West, the United States of America, its allies in Europe and their sphere of influence in the Pacific region; in the East, the Soviet Union which supported the communists in China and extended its sphere of influence to the regions struggling against Western colonialism. The dividing line between the two cut through Germany, Korea, Indochina and the Middle East. The world war had hardly ended when already signs of the coming cold war appeared.

The *West* had created the basis of its future influence by the monetary agreements of Bretton Woods in 1944, regulating the economy and trade relations in the post-war world. These were not signed by the Soviet Union. From 1947, the reconstruction and economic development of West Europe were taken care of by the American Marshall plan. Treaties of defence and mutual assistance further fortified the bloc — NATO (the North Atlantic Treaty Organization), the European Council and ANZUS, the security pact between the USA, Australia and New Zealand.

In the *East* the COMECON (a council for mutual economic assistance) and the Warsaw Pact strengthened links in the Soviet bloc. Mao Tse-Tung (Mao Zedong) proclaimed the People's Republic of China in 1949, and a year later the Soviet Union and China signed a pact of mutual assistance. From 1952 onwards the German Democratic Republic began to build the "iron curtain".

A first *confrontation of power* took place with the Soviet blockade of West Berlin in 1948 to which the USA responded by flying in supplies to the besieged city for almost a year. The tension also led to local wars in which the big powers became involved. The whole Middle East became an explosive region, not only because of the creation of the state of Israel in 1948 and the plight of Palestinian refugees, but also through the struggle for influence in the oil-producing countries. In Korea the civil war of 1950-53 threatened to intensify into another world war as United Nations troops, most of them from the US, faced a direct intervention by the Chinese army. In Indochina France became involved in a losing colonial war. The USA claimed world leadership, promising help to all who fought the eastern bloc. In some Western nations there was an obsessive fear of the growing communist power. Both power blocs strove to extend their zone of influence in the Caribbean and Central and South America where outside economic and political interests began to dictate national policies.

While this power struggle went on, *movements of revolt and national liberation* steadily gathered momentum. A number of independent states appeared on the scene of world history, refusing to align themselves to either of the two blocs. In 1947 India, Pakistan and Ceylon (Sri Lanka) became independent, soon followed by Burma and Indonesia. British interests were challenged in Egypt and Iran, as were French and Spanish dominance in North Africa, with war breaking out in Algeria. In other parts of Africa, too, there were movements of revolt against European domination, such as the Mau Mau in Kenya. The non-aligned movements and nations met for the first time in 1955 at an Afro-Asiatic conference in Bandung. "The voiceless people of the world have found their voice again," declared the Indonesian president.

Although the international power struggle affected almost all people around the globe, its impact on *daily life* varied from region to region and from one social class to another. In many Asian, African and Latin American villages, life continued very much as before 1946. In former areas of war the concern for reconstruction dominated all else. In North America and other regions that had not gone through the upheaval of war, consumer societies grew with a steady rise in material living standards. People became more mobile with the rapid increase in transportation facilities. As Western Europe recovered from the ravages of war it gradually joined this consumer society.

The world war had resulted in revolutionary *scientific discoveries* and inventions, especially in the realm of armaments. New technologies led to a new industrial revolution. In 1946 the first electronic computer was constructed. The invention of transistors led to a quick development of portable radios, televisions and smaller computers. Around 1950 only a minority of people could afford a TV set and thus have access to TV programmes. Books, newspapers, radio, gramophone and cinema were still the most popular media of information and entertainment.

What at that time marked the life of people even more than the growing use of the products of new scientific discoveries was what has been called the *revolution of rising expectations*. Many hoped that through such discoveries and new technologies poverty could be overcome, diseases cured and the well-being of people promoted.

Kraemer wanted to see together this orb and the cross. Where was God acting, through judgment and grace, in the post-war world? Where did the gospel require Christian believers to speak and act prophetically, affirming or challenging trends in world history? To which service should they commit themselves? And, above all, how could they be equipped for such a presence in the world? These were the questions with which the work at the Ecumenical Institute began.

A difficult beginning

Now that the official opening was over, the Ecumenical Institute could begin its work. The dignitaries had left. After the inauguration Kraemer had to go back to Holland. Earlier commitments and ill health did not allow him to take up his new assignment in Bossey before January 1948. The chairman and secretary of the executive board, Robert C. Mackie and Willem A. Visser 't Hooft, were more than busy; they had to pass on the work of the World Student Christian Federation to a new generation of leaders, and also prepare for the first World Council of Churches assembly. A warden had been appointed for the Ecumenical Institute, Henry-Louis Henriod, a former general secretary of the World Student Christian Federation, who lived in a chalet close to the château. He was responsible for community life and administration. A housekeeper had just started work. There still was no qualified interpreter, and volunteers from among the participants had to help with the work.

As already mentioned the château was ill-equipped as a training centre. Five or six beds could go into the large rooms on the second and third floors, but this was not a satisfactory arrangement. Some rooms in the farm "Grande Coudre", ten minutes' walk from Bossey, were rented out for nine months. A beautiful 18th-century country house near the château was bought in the summer of 1947 — *"Petit Bossey"*. It was once a private boarding school, established by the owner, Jean-Pierre Vaucher, a well-known Genevese professor of botany and church history and in that sense a worthy predecessor for the interdisciplinary study conferences that were to be held at the Institute. With Petit Bossey there was now sufficient accommodation for the participants of the early courses. However, the château still had no chapel, and no adequate kitchen, library and lecture hall.

Nevertheless, ecumenical education could now begin. Suzanne de Diétrich, the only resident lecturer, had to shoulder much of the responsibility for the *first ten-week course* for which 37 lay people had gathered from 15 nations. The executive board had hastily prepared a far too crowded programme with outstanding speakers. Over two hundred hours of lectures and seminars were scheduled. Some forty of these concentrated on currents of thought and developments in the post-war world, with leaders such as the Russian Orthodox philosopher Nicolas Berdyaev and the American social ethicist John Bennett in charge. About forty hours were devoted to the life of the churches and another forty to the vocation of the laity; among the speakers for these were, besides Adolf Keller and Visser 't Hooft, persons like the German Lutherans Reinold von Thadden and Hanns Lilje and the British Anglican Oliver Tomkins. The main emphasis of the programme was on Bible study, which included some eighty hours of introduction and exegesis, led mainly by Suzanne but also by the Swiss Old and New Testament scholars Walter Zimmerli and Pierre Bonnard. Except for Suzanne, and for a few weeks von Thadden, all these resource persons could be at Bossey only for a few hours or days.

There was enough, perhaps too much, intellectual and spiritual food. Yet the deepest level of ecumenical education could not be dealt with in the lecture room. "During this first Bossey course, and most of the following, the struggle to become 'a true community' has been the hardest of all," observed Suzanne, who wrote about the first group of participants: "Many of these men and women had gone through hard war experiences. There was a Dutch officer and his wife who had both spent three years in a Japanese prisoners' camp without ever being able to communicate with each other; a Czech who had spent nearly six years in concentration camps in Germany; a French girl who was at the point of death when the Swedish Red Cross rescued her from Ravensbrück; a Norwegian girl who had lost sleep working and travelling every night for the resistance movement. And there were the Germans, coming from their bombed cities, often unaware of what others had gone through, suffering from an all-too-long mental isolation."

Information and knowledge about the world, the experience of the churches during the war and the growing ecumenical movement and a new understanding of the role of lay people — all these were very much needed after the isolation behind closed frontiers. Yet this had to be accompanied by a *process of healing*, of "detoxification", and liberation from the captivity of ideologies and prejudices. To discover the human being in the erstwhile enemy one had to go through a painful struggle, passing from anger and resentment through conversion and confession, reaching at last a costly reconciliation. Many participants found it hard to speak to one another, not just because of language difficulties but because they were still feeling too deeply hurt to expose themselves in an honest exchange.

Regular meals, restful sleep and the Bossey environment contributed to this healing process. Participants had to do manual work for

[handwritten: The 1st came to the war —]

[handwritten: diff forms of ecumenism :]

at least an hour a day in the garden or the house. Even if they could not — or did not yet want to — enter into a deep conversation, they could together saw wood for the common fire, prepare food for the common meal or wash the dishes. Such corporate manual work helped to build the community more than lectures on reconciliation. It remained part of all the early Bossey courses.

The executive board had hoped to have *Reinold von Thadden* as a resident lecturer for Bossey. This layman from an old German family had played an important role in the student movement and the Confessing Church struggle against Hitler. As an officer in the German army in occupied Belgium he had at great personal risk saved many from the atrocities of the Nazi special police force. Towards the end of the war he became a prisoner and was sent to Siberia. In this Russian prison camp he founded the nucleus of what became the German "Kirchentag", the large gathering of church members and others seeking encouragement and strength for a true Christian presence in the modern world. Because of ill health and increasing responsibilities for the Kirchentag von Thadden could not accept full-time work at the Ecumenical Institute. He nevertheless spent several weeks helping with the first course and lectured with authority on the ministry of the laity. Those who had suffered from German occupation during the war met in him somebody whom they could deeply respect.

According to the testimonies of participants at that first course, the other healing person was *Suzanne de Diétrich*. A walking stick in each hand, this small, physically handicapped woman came down in the morning from her second-floor room in the château to remain in her office and the dining/lecture room on the ground floor till late at night. Her unfailing presence, her readiness to listen, and her animation of Bible studies became the heart of Bossey. She did not gloss over tension and anger but discreetly helped the group to deal on its own with enmity and guilt and to search for a new community. Through the daily Bible studies she made sure that in personal and corporate meetings and conversations there was always a third presence, that of God speaking through the prophets, apostles and Jesus.

Bible study was done according to different methods. Sometimes participants were asked to spend the first half-hour reading and meditating on the assigned text individually. Then it was examined in small groups, led by participants whom Suzanne had briefed with necessary background information and leading questions. This led to a plenary session, with the exchange of questions and discoveries, where Suzanne summed up the insights gained in the corporate study and shared with the participants what she herself had learned through meditation on the passage. At other times a biblical theme would be chosen, such as peace or salvation, or a biblical image like the vine, the building or the body. Suzanne would then introduce this theme or image, show the correlations between the Old and the New Testament and assign different texts for study in groups. This might again lead to a plenary session.

Whatever method was followed, *corporate Bible studies* formed the backbone of early Bossey courses. Usually five whole mornings a week were devoted to them. It was never a Bible study for its own sake. Always the biblical message was placed in the context of pressing world issues and the tasks faced by the churches in their search for greater faithfulness. Kraemer told the central committee of the World Council: "Perhaps the most influential part of the work of the Institute lies in the study of the Bible carried on in the courses, during which the Bible is read to ascertain the word of God for our time."

One difficulty which in later years strongly hampered the work of Bossey was little felt during the early period, namely that of *finance*. The grant of US$500,000 was wisely administered. It covered the rent for the château as well as the price of Petit Bossey; it also provided, for some eight years, more than ninety percent of the annual budget — salaries, subsidies for board and lodging and for travel, upkeep, etc. The plan was for the World Council gradually to include the running costs of Bossey in its regular budget. Moreover, the WCC committee on interchurch aid helped with an increasing amount for scholarships. Also other gifts were sought and received. The annual budget of $65,000 (at that time worth about SFr.278,200) was usually under-spent. In 1952 this budget could even be reduced to $60,000 without substantially reducing the work of the Institute.

Courses and conferences

The original Bossey programme for a year included three *long training courses*, each of around two and a half months. They were meant, in the first place, for lay people, but already for the second one, in early 1947, young pastors and theological students were also invited to participate. Hans Hoekendijk, just back from missionary service in Indonesia, led that course together with Suzanne. It is remembered especially for a memorable session with Reinhold Niebuhr on international politics. In the same year two other long training sessions were held, one for youth leaders with 52 participants from 22 nations, and the other for lay people studying the theme of the inaugural assembly of the World Council which was to be held in Amsterdam. Among its resource persons were M.M. Thomas from India and the Russian Orthodox thinker Paul Evdokimov. In the following long course Martin Niemöller, the prophet of the Confessing Church in Germany, and Eberhardt Müller, the founder of the Evangelical Academy of Bad Boll, were the main speakers. The theme was evangelism because Kraemer felt that "the Christian church has to rethink and revise her missionary and evangelistic task entirely in view of the atmosphere and conditions of the modern world".

Such longer courses continued until 1950. Two years earlier the executive board had suggested a *shift of emphasis* for the programme. Serious ecumenical training needed a longer period, preferably a whole semester. Keller's dream of a graduate school for ecumenical studies thus surfaced again. Moreover, lay people in secular professions found it difficult to obtain leave of absence for two or three months. The demand for shorter courses and more specialized conferences was growing. It was felt that the work should now concentrate on gathering lay people of the same profession and on interdisciplinary conferences to address important issues in the world and the churches. General ecumenical education could continue in shorter summer courses.

In 1947 Suzanne brought together *leaders of lay training*, who had founded the European centres and associations mentioned earlier, to help church members to be present as Christians in their daily work and world. "They are bubbling with ideas and projects!" she wrote. It must indeed have been a remarkable gathering of pioneers. One of the first Bossey publications came out of this meeting: "Professional Life as Christian Vocation". The group made proposals and submitted requests to the World Council in process of formation. Bossey was asked to become the clearing house for these lay centres and movements. The directors of lay training, soon including participants from outside Europe, met annually at Bossey in the following six years. The assembly at Amsterdam was asked to include in its programme a committee on the "Significance of the Laity in the Church" and to establish a secretariat, with a travelling secretary, for this work.

Most of the specialized meetings of the early period were gatherings of *lay people of the same profession*

— Teachers met often from 1947 onwards. They examined the relationships between education and humanism, between confessional and secular schools, among state, church and school. They also discussed how subjects like science or geography could be taught and how far Christian faith might influence such teaching.

— Medical doctors came annually to Bossey under the direction of the Geneva doctor Paul Tournier. The Bossey staff increasingly participated in the preparation of these gatherings and expanded their scope of discussion beyond personal medical ethics to the study of structural problems in the nursing profession.

— People involved in industry met annually, beginning in 1948. They concentrated on the dilemmas of decision-making by managers and trade union leaders as well as on human relationships within a production-oriented industry. Suzanne reported: "We found that the deeper down men are in the problems of this world, the more thirsty they are for true spiritual refreshment, for simple and fraternal Christian living." In such professional meetings also the programme included regular Bible studies.

— It was more difficult to get artists together, yet twice they met at Bossey: a mixed group of musicians, poets, playwrights, actors, painters, sculptors and a few theologians and thinkers especially sensitive to the voice of the arts. "Such a group has always a charm of its own because there is much to see, to listen to, much gaiety and freedom!", the report recalls, but also adds that the artists felt rather lost with the theological introductions.

— Similar professional meetings brought together people involved in politics, young lawyers, journalists and social workers.

Another type of specialized conferences dealt with *issues in the modern world* which had to be brought to the attention of the churches because of the implications for their ministry in the world.

— A good example was the study on social welfare. For several months Paul Abrecht from the World Council headquarters staff worked half-time for Bossey and helped with this. First, a small consultation with experts surveyed the consequences of new trends in secular welfare work. This led to a series of more specialized

Left: The abbey of Notre Dame de Bonmont

Below: The old tower of Bossey

Photos WCC

Petit Bossey

Above: Adolf Keller
Right: J. H. Oldham

Willem Visser 't Hooft lecturing to students

Hendrik Kraemer and Suzanne de Diétrich

Hans-Heinrich Wolf, second from right, with a group of students

conferences with social workers and social schools, taking up subjects such as the welfare state, delinquent youth, prison and prisoners.

— A similar series of conferences focused on the family. After a more general meeting, a small group of experts initiated a study on the controversial question of birth control for which extensive documentation was gathered. This led to a larger meeting on the church and marriage. The role of "eros" in modern society was positively and negatively evaluated, for instance through Bible studies on the Song of Songs, and the uncritical identification of Western patterns of family life with the biblical view on marriage was challenged.

— Bossey's continuing contact with leaders of lay training led to the study on the meaning of work. This had become a crucial issue for J.H. Oldham who played a prominent role in the first Bossey conference on this theme. The study process led to the sixth section of the WCC assembly at Evanston on "The Laity — the Christian in His Vocation".

The most demanding of Bossey meetings were the *interdisciplinary conferences*.

— A consultation on the meaning of history was organized with the university commission of the World Student Christian Federation. It brought together historians, philosophers of history and theologians. Graeco-Roman historiography and Chinese and Indian conceptions of history were looked at in the light of Old and New Testament perspectives and the views of church fathers on history. Where was history leading to? That was indeed a question of great urgency in the post-war world.

— A conference with sociologists and theologians examined the significance of sociology for the strategy of the church. Kraemer said, in introducing this gathering: "It is organized not because we believe that sociology is *the* way, or even *a* way, to salvation, but because we are strongly convinced that social research is one of the instruments given to us to understand more adequately the significance of social relationships and institutions." He added that churches and church leaders were still largely unaware of this means to self-knowledge and realistic self-criticism, at the same time pointing to the need for theology to challenge sociology.

— Similar interdisciplinary conferences brought together biologists and theologians and philosophers and theologians.

These professional and interdisciplinary meetings added an important dimension to the conferences which dealt more directly with *the churches' life, mission and renewal*. Subjects taken up were the churches' relationships with the people of Israel, the church and rural life. One of the conferences dealt with ecumenism on the local level. Another, on pastoral care, brought together professors of pastoral theology, psychiatrists and pastors/priests for discussing why so many people tend to turn to the doctor rather than to the pastor when seeking help in their problems of daily life. What implications did this have for theological training?

More general ecumenical education happened mainly in *the large summer courses*.

— A theological student course met annually from 1948 onwards (two to three weeks). Subjects taken up were often those of the WCC study department, such as the authority of the Bible for today. One course centred on a critique of democracy and another on questions of communication.

— From 1948 an annual (usually two weeks) course was held for pastors and/or missionaries. Ordained and lay professional church workers were introduced to the insights gained in the field of the ministry of the laity in the world. As relatively few persons from Asia, Africa and Latin America could participate in early Bossey meetings, the large courses for missionaries on furlough became especially important. What had been learned at the Ecumenical Institute was thereby disseminated in many areas of the world, often in regions with which the official ecumenical movement had little or no contact.

— Vacation courses for lay people (usually one to two weeks) replaced the earlier long training sessions. The Bossey staff were also fully involved in the large European laymen's meeting at Bad Boll in 1951 and, to a lesser degree, in the North American laymen's meeting at Buffalo a year later.

A very special ecumenical education exercise was the annual *Berlin courses*. As the East-West tension grew, ever fewer participants from Eastern Europe could come to Bossey: the East German government blocked all visas — because of the Rockefeller grant the Ecumenical Institute was considered as part of capitalist propaganda.

Bossey and friends in Eastern Germany responded by organizing extension work. Since 1951 a small team of the Institute consisting of members of the teaching staff and later also Graduate School students annually went to Berlin to conduct two or three short Bossey courses. All who participated in these teams remember those weeks as a tiring but rewarding and spiritually enriching learning experience.

Priorities and transformations

In 1949 the Ecumenical Institute had its first critical evaluation. Meetings were held and long memoranda written on the "future of Bossey" — an exercise it would undergo periodically in coming decades.

The following were the reasons why decisions about priorities had to be made:

— The programme was growing beyond the capacity of both the house and the staff. Courses for ecumenical education, each with its own theme, already took up four to five months of the year. Annually there were five or more specialized conferences for professional groups or interdisciplinary meetings on frontier issues. These often involved preliminary consultations and/or travel as well as multicopied or printed reports.

— The château had been rented out only for five years, and the lease expired in 1951. The number of participants had gone up. The château had to be bought and transformed to accommodate more people or a larger place had to be found.

— The Bossey staff felt overburdened. Looking at the programme and the work conditions during the first five years, one cannot help wondering how so much could be achieved with just two resident teaching staff! The help from the WCC headquarters and the contribution of short-time visiting lecturers were welcome, but preparing for specialized conferences took several months and ecumenical education courses called for a continuing staff presence. No wonder that Kraemer and Suzanne had constantly to live and work with "a healthy dissatisfaction".

Two unpublished papers, circulated for discussion, outline two *different directions for the future* of the Ecumenical Institute. They express not only personal views but echo opinions voiced in World Council governing bodies and in the Bossey board which, from 1948, was chaired by Reinold von Thadden.

Visser 't Hooft's memorandum of May 1949 says:

Precisely at a time when the World Council of Churches takes on its definitive character as an organ of the churches themselves, there is the great need for a body which, while directly related to the World Council, has nevertheless considerable freedom of action and can thus enter into new fields of thought and action with which the churches are as yet unfamiliar. It might thus be said that the Ecumenical Institute is the most important energizing centre of the World Council of Churches.

He reported on the use made of the Rockefeller grant and reviewed the present and future financial situation. He proposed that the château be bought and the needed facilities added. For this a sum of $250,000 would be needed. Only with a permanent home could the Ecumenical Institute continue to give the students "a new vision of their Christian task in the modern world... and remain a source of constant enrichment to the World Council and its member churches".

Suzanne's memorandum of August 1949 expressed her deep commitment to the work of the Institute but questioned the wisdom of acquiring the château. The necessary funds for buying and transforming the place could probably be found, but would the churches be able to continue to pay for the running costs and upkeep of such a large centre? Suzanne feared that future circumstances might necessitate a reduction in the area of scholarships and staff appointments in order to hold on to the building. A reserve of at least two million dollars might well be needed. Her hesitations went beyond the financial reasons. She felt that the château was "of another age", not in keeping with the simple style of life which true ecumenism advocates. For serving the world, and not just Europe, another way of work was called for. Could not Petit Bossey be transformed to become the centre of the Ecumenical Institute and for hosting specialized conferences of some thirty participants? It would then be possible to set apart more money for scholarships and appoint a larger, mobile staff to do ecumenical extension work in different continents.

Where did wisdom lie? Even at this distance of almost fifty years it is difficult to judge. Had Suzanne's proposals been followed the World Council would today not own the château. The Graduate School of Ecumenical Studies, its relationship to Geneva university and its rich harvest of graduates all over the world — all these would hardly have developed as they did. However, Bossey history since 1970 shows that Suzanne's fears were at many points justified.

Financial difficulties increasingly crippled creative initiatives and extension work remained on the agenda of the Institute but was never fully developed.

After another visit of Visser 't Hooft to the Rockefeller Centre, *a second Rockefeller grant* was announced. This settled the matter. In July 1950 the World Council bought the château. Renovation and related work started in February 1951 and was completed in early 1952. During that period Bossey courses and conferences took place in three other conference centres: at Bièvres near Paris, at Woudschoten near Utrecht and at Gwatt near Bern.

The changes made in the château meant that the large rooms on the second and third floors were converted into single rooms. On the ground floor the Salon blanc, formerly the dining room, became a sitting room for informal gatherings. The Salon vert and Salon brun were transformed to become respectively the library, a reading room and offices. An entrance hall, with large windows, now connected the château to two separate buildings: the Colombie and the Orangerie. The former accommodated a kitchen, staff quarters and a dormitory. Heating was installed in the latter and the large space sub-divided to become the dining room and the lecture hall. A special gift was received to install facilities there for simultaneous interpretation. The old, crumbling chalet where the Henriods had lived was replaced by a modern building, the "Dépendance". Together with Petit Bossey the Institute could now accommodate some eighty people. Suzanne, who took a lively interest in all this and made many suggestions, was quite pleased with the outcome and wrote: "Snoring and sleepless gentlemen can now be sure of getting a single room."

Still there was no adequate *housing for the staff*. A third gift from Rockefeller made it possible to build the director's villa and a duplex for two staff families. The lecture hall had to serve also as the place of worship, but plans were underway for transforming the old winepress into a chapel.

Other significant transformations, not in brick and mortar, took place in the early 1950s. A *survey of participants* indicated that during the first three years 443 persons attended courses and conferences organized by Bossey. They came from 45 countries and 15 different denominations, though the majority were still Europeans and Protestants. From 1952 onwards the number increased considerably.

National correspondents in all parts of the world, usually secretaries of national councils of churches, helped with the recruitment. Some courses were now attended by eighty people, with an increasing number from beyond Europe and more Orthodox and Roman Catholic representatives. With so many and such diverse participants it was difficult to maintain the high level of personal encounter and participation which had characterized the early Bossey meetings. The popularity of the course for theological students and the annual graduate school meant that the number of theologically trained persons increased while proportionally fewer lay people in secular professions now attended the meetings.

With the growing number of participants and the increasing diversity of work *the permanent staff team* had to be expanded. Adequate simultaneous interpretation was needed and the office had to be organized. Two persons began these tasks with much competence.

— In 1949 Visser 't Hooft sent his Genevese secretary Simone Mathil to Bossey for a few weeks to help reorganize the rather chaotic office of the Institute. She stayed on for twenty-four years until her retirement. With her competence and firm will she kept the administration in order. Both students and staff respected her for her commitment and service. Children on the campus had an understanding advocate in her when they had got into trouble over some mischief or other.

— A participant of the second lay course, Ilse Friedeberg, demonstrated extraordinary gifts for simultaneous interpretation and she became the first full-time interpreter. With her capacity to take notes at the same time, she could tell students after the sessions what the lecturers really had been trying to say. A German Lutheran, she had a deep affinity with Orthodox worship and spirituality, and she helped Orthodox participants to fit into a still mainly Protestant milieu.

— Others joined the growing permanent staff: a gardener, a chauffeur, a second full-time interpreter, a librarian, and office secretaries.

More attention had to be given to *the welcoming of participants and their welfare*.

— In his role as warden, Henry-Louis Henriod had become a fatherly friend for many. Those who attended the early Bossey courses remember how carefully he cut out participants' profiles in black paper. Instead of group photographs these silhouettes were put up on the walls of the rooms in the château, competing with the many pictures of Napoleon. In 1951 Henriod reached retirement age.

— A year later Renée Sturm was appointed as the first hostess or "châtelaine". Though she stayed only for a few years, she left her permanent mark on life in Bossey by starting the tradition of the blue angels. Dressed in blue overalls these teenagers served as volunteers, usually for six months. One cannot imagine Bossey now without them — in recent years, young men as well as young women. The blue overalls disappeared long ago and "angels" tend to appear now in blue jeans.

A few of those who occasionally came from the Geneva staff or from abroad as *helpers in teaching* have already been mentioned. Two more need to be added. In 1949 S.S. Selvaratnam, the founder of a Christian ashram in Jaffna, Ceylon, stayed for several months at Bossey. His radiant personality made a deep impression on both staff and participants.

After the Amsterdam assembly the World Council created a secretariat for laymen's work which was closely linked with the Ecumenical Institute. For a year Denis Baly, a British geographer with experience in the Middle East, worked for this secretariat.

A non-resident part-time staff member played an important role: *Hans-Hermann Walz* from the German academy of Bad Boll, who became laity secretary at the WCC headquarters. With his academy experience and his background of studies in law and theology, he gave guidance to the growing ecumenical rediscovery of the ministry of the laity and helped the Institute both in lay training and in interdisciplinary conferences. Although he did not live on the campus, Walz worked in a more than half-time capacity as the first assistant director of the Institute.

The period of the team of pioneers came to an end. Suzanne left the Institute in late 1954 to "retire" — and did Bossey extension work on her own through travels and teaching in Europe, North and Latin America and Africa. Kraemer had wanted to leave at the same time but was persuaded by the board to stay on until the summer of 1955. He then continued his ministry of teaching and writing in North America and Holland.

From a winepress to a chapel

In the 15th century Bossey had a chapel dedicated to Our Lady, but it had disappeared, like many other ancient buildings. Four centuries later Elisabeth Lange received special papal permission for mass to be celebrated at Bossey and in the medieval tower a chapel had been set apart for this. That place of worship had also disappeared by the time the Council took over the domain of Bossey.

There are church buildings in the neighbourhood. In the parish church of Céligny pastor Arnold Mobbs, who had helped Keller with the Geneva ecumenical seminars, specially welcomed the participants of Bossey meetings when he saw them at Sunday services, and often gave them English or German summaries of his sermons. Many links developed between the Institute and this local church.

Half an hour's walk to the south-west brings one to the small chapel of Chavannes-de-Bogis which had already played a role in ecumenical history. The summer conference of the World Student Christian Federation met in 1934 at nearby La Châtaigneraie, and it was in that chapel that conference participants gathered for a series of liturgical evening prayers. Probably for the first time in ecumenical history an international and interconfessional group had attempted here to share the rich liturgical tradition of different Christian confessions.

These *liturgical evening prayers* of 1934 anticipated much of the worship life of the Ecumenical Institute and they had two direct links with Bossey:

— Early international student meetings generally followed a Protestant, revivalist pattern of worship. The Student Federation decided to break with this tradition, but at that time fully ecumenical worship books were not available. Suzanne, then a Federation secretary, was asked to prepare the liturgies for those evening services at Chavanne-de-Bogis. She went into a private retreat with a pile of existing Orthodox, Roman Catholic, Anglican and various Protestant worship books, and produced the worship sheets in three languages.

— That first attempt to worship together through the great classical prayers and hymns of Christ's church led later to the publication of the Federation prayer and worship book *Venite Adoremus*. Together with the ecumenical hymnal *Cantate Domino* this prayer book played a large part in the whole worship life at Bossey during its first decades.

peruse via laity.

A report of the Institute's board comments on the experience of worship at Bossey:

> Numbers of people already think with gratitude of the Institute as the place at which they experienced most deeply the pain of the division of the church in its worship and the joy of entering into the richness of traditions other than their own. The deepening of worship there takes its place alongside the biblical revival and the rediscovery of the vocation of the laity, as the third aspect of the renewal of the church which the Institute can serve. Worship at an ecumenical centre should not be regarded as being primarily an education in comparative liturgics. It is in the first place the worship of the Almighty God.

The same report adds that there must also be space for "more private and personal forms of Christian devotion".

A place for both corporate and private worship was sorely lacking during the first five years of the Institute. The changes made at the château foresaw the building of *a chapel for the Institute*. What better and more symbolic place could have been found than the former winepress adjacent to the medieval tower? The World Council had never so far attempted to build a place of worship where representatives from all Christian confessions could feel at home. Much thought therefore went into the planning of this chapel. The large stone walls as well as the old wooden ceiling beams of the winepress building were preserved, and the base of the tower became part of the chapel. Decisions about the place and form of the altar were made after long discussion. From the outset it was clear that there should be *one* altar, and that it should be a simple, unadorned table which could be placed either against the wall or further out according to the particular confessional tradition. But which wall? The architects had suggested placing it near the side wall towards the lake. This was rejected. According to ancient Christian tradition the altar found its place at the centre of the head wall towards the East with a movable pulpit and a movable lectern at the left and right side. A special committee was appointed to suggest further interior arrangements, but for several years the chapel remained without any further additions. It was inaugurated on 1 November 1952, a month after the beginning of the first Graduate School.

At times the chapel was crowded. This was especially the case in the summer of 1953 when the great theological path-finders were at Bossey working on the main theme for the WCC assembly at Evanston, and when *famous preachers* led the service. Walz wrote about this occasion:

> In the chapel, as in the ancient church and still in some Eastern Orthodox churches, the people have stood crowded cheek by jowl. It is a good thing that instead of St Augustine or Chrysostomos preaching for two if not more hours, Karl Barth or Georges Florovsky, John Baillie or Anders Nygren have been in the pulpit with an awareness in their minds of the saddening fact that modern men are not able to listen longer than twenty minutes.

For most of the time the chapel was the place for a worshipping community. Whether there were any guests at Bossey or not, during these early years many of the resident team gathered there each day for morning prayer and a regular, brief period of intercession at noon. During courses and conferences a third daily service was held in the evening.

The Graduate School of Ecumenical Studies

In 1950 the Bossey board discussed the future of *long training courses* for lay people. Some felt that the Institute should concentrate even more strongly on professional and interdisciplinary conferences, others pleaded for much longer courses. The minutes record: "In this connection Dr Müller proposed that a real semester for students should be organized. Thus there should be held a semester for medical students, another for law students, another one for theological students. This suggestion was favoured by several members." The board asked the directors to make concrete proposals, and soon afterwards a staff memorandum was submitted suggesting that from 1952 onwards a fully academic and longer training course of 4-5 months be held. "The first group to be invited should be composed of theological students together with laymen who had a university background. At a later stage it might be possible to hold similar courses for students of other faculties."

Discussion on this memorandum at the meeting of the board in early 1951 was introduced by Jaques Courvoisier, the dean of the theological faculty of Geneva university. He reminded the board of the fact that as early as the 1930s ecumenical seminars had been held in Geneva. He said that when the theological faculty had heard about the Bossey plans it had immediately taken up the matter with the university and the Geneva authorities. Two draft documents were presented to the board, one for legal purposes and the other describing the character of such a graduate institute related to the university. Courvoisier became the key person for relationships between Bossey and the Geneva faculty. Thanks to his efforts the Graduate School of Ecumenical Studies could start in 1952 itself, with a greater academic status and the power to grant a degree. Perhaps the takeover by professional theologians happened a little too quickly. During the first half of 1951 Kraemer was on a long visit to Asia and he could not participate in the discussions. The ambitious project proposed in 1950, which would have maintained the strong emphasis on the vocation of lay people in their secular professions, was in fact never fully considered and soon forgotten.

The WCC central committee approved in 1951 the joint venture of Bossey with the Geneva theological faculty. A *board of the Graduate School* was appointed whose members were all men and all theological professors. The first chairman, C.T. Craig from Great Britain, died a year after he took over, and Courvoisier became the moderator of the board, continuing in that capacity until the late 1960s. Other prominent members were E. Schlink from Germany, W. Horton from the USA, B. Ioannidis from Greece, D.G. Moses from India and Visser 't Hooft who from the outset showed much interest in this new venture. The board had to spend a great deal of time on details of the complex relationships between the World Council, the Graduate School and Geneva university via the autonomous theological faculty. Also, the tasks of the board of the Institute and the new board for the Graduate School needed to be clarified. Above all, the aims and functions of this new enterprise had to be defined and the teaching programme for the first semesters determined.

The *aims* of the Graduate School were announced as follows:

(a) To offer an opportunity during a semester of four and a half months for concentrated study, in regular academic fashion, of the problems of ecumenism. (b) To show what are historical and theological obstacles to unity. (c) To show how present-day activities of the ecumenical movement, based as they are on a deepened conception of the nature and vocation of the church, affect the thought and conduct of the individual churches. (d) To create a community of work and life among the students, the teaching staff and the other residents of the house.

Those students who satisfactorily completed the course would receive the *certificate* of the school. Graduates who continued research on a specific ecumenical subject and whose research papers were accepted would be granted *ecumenical diplomas* jointly by the school and the theological faculty. Plans for creating an ecumenical *doctoral programme* as well in connection with the Graduate School were already in an advanced stage. Kraemer, as the dean of the school, was nominated as an honorary professor at the Geneva faculty.

The *first semester* from October 1952 to February 1953 was a difficult one. The original plan was to accept only up to twenty students and to conduct, alongside the academic course, other Bossey meetings. Kraemer had pleaded that only well-qualified graduates be accepted and that the studies concentrate on one general subject. The board was less strict in accepting candidates and prepared a far too diverse programme. Finally 24 students of very different age groups from 13 nationalities and ten different church traditions came, mainly Lutherans and Reformed, but also four Eastern Orthodox, an Old Catholic and a priest of the Mar Thoma Church. All but two of these participants had already studied theology, but their academic standards were far too diverse.

The *teaching programme* was to consist of about twenty classes a week, and often tutorials in the evenings. There were courses on the history and problems of the ecumenical movement, several series of lectures on the church, for instance the church in the New Testament, its search through the centuries for unity and renewal, its theology of mission. Two Christian confessional families were presented, Lutheran and Orthodox. Four lecture series concentrated on movements of thought and life in contemporary Christianity in Asia, Great Britain, the USA and the European continent. Considerable time was given to social ethics and a Christian critique of capitalism, socialism and communism. In addition to this heavy lecture programme, planned for each week was a morning of Bible studies and two afternoons of seminars for which students had to prepare papers. Students had to pass written exams in several subjects. All except two received the certificate. Those who made the deepest impact among the lecturers and seminar leaders were D.T. Niles from Ceylon, Walter Freytag from Germany, Paul Evdokimov from France and Ronald Preston from Great Britain. Two lecturers from the USA, William Pauck and H.E. Short, stayed at Bossey for several months and thus became much more part of the learning community than those who came only for a few days or weeks.

"As the Graduate School progressed, we discovered more and more that, for all of us, the teaching staff, the staff of the Institute and the students themselves, it was *a far bigger experiment than we had anticipated*," wrote Kraemer in his report. "It is, in fact, entirely unlike any other activity of the Institute, and has to develop a style of its own." Students had to adapt themselves to a different diet, climate, environment and new mental attitudes. Language difficulties proved to be a great handicap. Worship, which should have been an expression of community life, became during the first months a subject of endless and paralyzing discussions. There were too many short-term lecturers. Students complained that with the wide range of subjects the lectures covered, they felt confused. Kraemer fell ill during the semester and for several weeks could not lead the course. Suzanne commented that in such a long academic course, with mainly theological students, the Bible did not play the same important role as in summer courses and that she had not found the right way of animating Bible study.

After this difficult beginning Kraemer wrote his *provisional conclusions* which are still worth reading. He proposed that the number of short-time lecturers should be reduced, that at least two professors must stay with the group for the whole period, that for each semester a full-time tutor should be found and that the dean of the Graduate School had to be relieved from responsibilities for all other Bossey programmes. This would obviously have financial implications; not only more scholarships were needed, but the Graduate School should have a budget of its own. Kraemer felt that, because of the need to promote real community life, only mature students should be accepted, and that academic qualifications should be higher than the two years of university studies now required. The library had to be improved. Future students should be given more detailed information about the special nature of the Graduate School.

The last provisional conclusion pointed to what later became a special feature of Bossey: "A striking experience has been that one of the best ways of making the students realize the depth and difficulty of the ecumenical movement is to confront them with *a study of Orthodoxy*." Kraemer proposed that for every semester there should be a resident Orthodox lecturer and that the study of Orthodoxy must become a regular part of the Graduate School.

The second and third semesters had less crowded teaching programmes, and some of the above recommendations were tested in practice. Both the board and the lecturers still saw the Graduate School mainly in terms of a European theological faculty. For many years — perhaps even today — this attempt of ecumenical education has remained in an experimental stage. For students and the staff the four and a half winter months became a difficult, often frustrating and yet at the same time a stimulating and challenging experience. All available reminiscences of participants of these early semesters testify to this. No one has suggested that the experiment should be stopped.

Bossey: a "seminary"

The Ecumenical Institute "is literally a 'seminary', *a place of sowing*", Kraemer told the WCC central committee. Sowing for the field of the whole oikoumene, the whole inhabited earth, is an impossible enterprise. The teaching staff almost from the beginning faced a series of tensions and dilemmas. These can hardly ever be solved, and as long as the Bossey experiment continues one must learn to live with them.

First there was the problem well known to all who teach, of finding the right balance between *preparatory study and teaching*. Sowers must search for good seed, lest they end up sowing chaff. Usually teachers specialize in a certain field, and teach within a given cultural context with methods generally accepted in that environment. This is not possible at Bossey. A number of subjects have to be tackled, and these have to be taught in an interconfessional and interdisciplinary way. This calls for an enormous amount of preparatory study, and usually it has to be done during nights and vacations. To make this possible, the board decided that during the first two months no meetings organized by the directors should be held at Bossey, so that the teaching staff would be relatively free to do serious preparatory work. It worked for two years, but then the full teaching programme squeezed out such free periods for study. A proposal to separate the function of the chief director from that of the dean of the Graduate School so that both would have some free time for study could not be implemented. The problem remained unsolved.

Secondly, a balance had to be found between *necessary visitation and necessary presence*. Those who sow must know the ground. For Bossey the ground is the whole world with its diversity of cultures, races, socio-economic, political and ecclesiastical situations. Great sensitivity to this many-faceted and changing world and some understanding of the background of those who come to meetings at the Institute are indispensable. These cannot be acquired through reading alone. They entail a fair amount of travelling and visitation. At the same time it is important that members of the teaching staff stay with the groups, become part of the learning and growing process. They must be present when the occasional crises crop up, as they do, especially at nights and on week-ends. The tension was strongly felt even in the early years, despite the fact that both Kraemer and Suzanne had long experience working in international and interconfessional situations. Not many of their successors could bring to the "seminary" such deep and comprehensive ecumenical experience.

A third tension grew between the *initiation and the follow-up of work*. Most professional and interdisciplinary conferences demanded that the explorations begun should be followed up by further study and meetings. Soon the Bossey programme began to grow like a snowball. Work had either to concentrate on a few subjects, which involved the risk of no longer being able to respond to new agenda points both of the world and the gospel, or constantly pioneer in new areas and later abandon them, thus becoming far too superficial. The directors and the board struggled with this dilemma without ever finding a satisfactory answer.

There was the related tension between the *involvement with ever-new learning communities and maintaining contact with former ones*. When the participants of the long lay training courses and of the Graduate Schools returned to their countries and local Christian communities they felt lonely and frustrated. The vision which they had received of the churches' worship and vocation in the world and the intense intercultural and interconfessional encounters which they had experienced were not shared by those back home with whom they now lived and worked. The Institute was asked to keep in touch with them, continuing to "feed" them through circular letters or by sending teams from Bossey for extension work. As early as 1949 Henriod went to Germany to meet with former students. During the Berlin courses there was always a day set apart for such a meeting, and sometimes up to a hundred former participants gathered. With the ever-growing number of persons who had passed through Bossey and their ever-wider geographic dispersion, the demand for maintaining contact could never be met satisfactorily.

There were signs of *tension between Bossey and the WCC head-quarters*. Up to the Evanston assembly in 1954 the World Council had remained a small and simple organization. Besides the General Secretariat there was the large Department of Reconstruction and Inter-Church Aid which helped Bossey with funding for scholarships. In addition to the Institute, there were only small secretariats, with not more than one executive secretary, for Faith and Order, Studies (mainly continuing the former Life and Work studies), Youth, and the Commission of the Churches for International Affairs which, like Bossey, had been created in 1946. There was much spontaneous collaboration among all these early WCC activities. However, as ever new concerns grew into full departments — as for instance those on evangelism, women, the laity — the danger grew of too much overlap between the work of Bossey and the new work now being initiated at the WCC headquarters. A firmer structure of work for the whole Council had yet to be created. As early as 1952, the Bossey board had long discussions on where the Institute should be located, in the General Secretariat or the proposed Division of Ecumenical Action. Those who pleaded for the first said "that the Institute with its ongoing life was basically different from other departments", and that it needed, like other educational institutions, a "far-reaching auton-omy". Others "warned against an independence which might put Bossey outside the normal life of the WCC and finally mean the weakening of its links with the churches". This tension has also remained unresolved.

Finally, the choice had to be made as to where to put the *main thrust of the Bossey programme*. Should it be on lay training for Christian presence in the world, or rather on the ecumenical education of theologically trained workers in the churches? The courses for theological students, pastors, priests and missionaries were by far the largest ones. The Graduate School also addressed itself in the first place to the churches' theologically trained workers. In fact by the early 1950s a shift had taken place. In official documents the cen-trality of lay training was still affirmed, and a good deal still happened in this field, but clearly the majority of participants were now theologically trained church workers, whether ordained or not. The "seminary" of the Ecumenical Institute certainly remained a place of sowing, but in the course of the ensuing decades it also took on characteristics of a "seminary" in the sense in which that term is usually understood.

This shift of emphasis in the Bossey programme was probably inevitable. Nevertheless, *Kraemer's warning* of 1954 still needs to be heard. He commented on the relationship between the "lay issue" and the renewal of the churches' life. According to him Bossey was not created for mobilizing ordinary church members for service in church activities. True, such a service of both laity and clergy was important. However, according to Kraemer the "lay issue" points to "the recovery of the fundamental point that the church is that body which is sent into the world and has a ministry to the world". It means "to confront lay Christians with the question what meaning and bearing the Christian faith has on the specific sector of life in which they spend the major part of their time and energy". They also must be confronted with the implications of Christian faith "on the great social, political, cultural, moral issues in which the world to which we all belong threatens to perish". Therefore "an ecumenical movement without a prophetic and persistent call towards renewal and reformation degenerates into 'organizing' ecclesiastical reunions without a renewed apprehension of the church as an instrument and demonstration of God's redemptive presence and action in this lost and forlorn world".

4. Growing Up and Reaching Out: 1955-1970

The basic directions for the work of the Ecumenical Institute had been set. There was still some money left over from the initial grants, and at the WCC assembly in Evanston the Council had assumed full responsibility for continuing this ecumenical laboratory. The major possibilities as well as the major difficulties for future experiments at Bossey had been explored. Now new managerial teams took over from the pioneers, and they were discerning new imperatives from the gospel, new ways of working with churches and the WCC headquarters, and new agenda points posed by the world. Within less than a decade life in the world had undergone many changes.

A fast-changing scene

Looking back on the events and developments from 1955 to 1970 one is struck by the effervescence of hopes and fears. The continuing *cold war* between the two power blocs left its mark on the life of people and nations. The Berlin wall, built in 1961 right through the former German capital, was a symbol of this. The arms race had steadily increased, and despite the warnings of scientists and against the appeals of peace conferences, it included the further development of nuclear weapons. Besides the USA and the Soviet Union, Great Britain, France and China now had atomic bombs. In 1956 on the Marshall Islands in Micronesia the USA tested the first transportable, immensely powerful hydrogen bomb, followed by France which tested similar bombs at Moruroa in Polynesia. When in 1962 the Soviet Union established a missile launching site in Cuba it risked the outbreak of another world war.

The rivalry between the power blocs manifested itself most strongly in the area of *space research*. In 1957 the Soviet Union launched Sputnik I, the very first satellite to orbit around the earth. Two years later the American satellite Explorer VI sent back photographs of the planet earth as seen from space. The widely publicized space exploration made a deep, worldwide impression. Seen from space the earth was beautiful; it was seen as one whole, without dividing walls and separate power blocs.

While competing world powers were busy exploring both the infinitely small atoms and the immensely large bodies in space, life and history continued on earth. The period was characterized by *rapid decolonization* and the emergence of new independent nations. Britain had to leave Egypt in 1956 and a year later Ghana declared independence. In the early 1960s almost all former colonies in Africa had become independent and the Organisation of African Unity was established at Addis Ababa. Tension grew in the Caribbean region when in 1959 Cuba joined the Eastern power bloc and began to support socialist revolutionary movements in the whole of Latin America. In Asia, the war continued in Indochina with growing US military involvement. The revolution in China penetrated ever more deeply and pervaded the total life of people. It led to the Sino-Soviet split and China's cultural revolution in 1966-68 in which the Red Book of Mao's thought was the gospel for shaping a new human being and a new society.

The time was marked by *a mood of unrest and confrontation*. In the East de-Stalinization began in 1956, the year that saw the popular uprising and its ruthless suppression in Hungary. Uprisings in Poland and Czechoslovakia in 1968 raised the hope that socialism with a human face would emerge — a hope crushed by Soviet tanks. In the West, the European Common Market was evolving and a West European parliament met for the first time in 1957. In the United States there was the growing struggle against racial discrimination and strong protests over American involvement in the Vietnam war. The Middle East continued to be an explosive region, with the Suez crisis in 1956, the Israeli-Arab war in 1967 and the growing Palestinian resistance movement.

Scientific discoveries, economic development and the growth of consumer societies in more and more regions of the world changed the *everyday life* of many. Transistor radios could now link even remote villages with the rest of the world. TV, tape recorders and audio-tapes were no longer the privilege of a few. Popular singers became the idols and prophets of youth in many parts of the world. The availability of birth control pills revolutionized sexual ethics. The first heart transplantation had been made. The genetic code was discovered, which opened the possibility for genetic manipulation. The ravages of tropical illnesses could now be checked by new medicines, better hygiene and new agricultural technologies. Nuclear power plants provided cheap electricity, though the problem of eliminating nuclear waste remained unsolved. Computers became smaller, more powerful and increasingly indispensable. No wonder that with all these developments — acclaimed by many as progress — the explosion of hopes continued. Organizations such as UNESCO fostered intercultural exchange and it appeared the world was on the way to becoming the global village.

By the 1960s *the other side of progress* had begun to manifest itself. Nuclear accidents happened from time to time. Pesticides proved to be a mixed blessing. New medicines sometimes had unforeseen adverse effects as in the case of thalidomide. The decline in infant mortality led to increasing overpopulation in several poor areas in Africa, Asia and Latin America. In Western societies, especially in North America, the hippie movement represented the revolt of young people against the meaninglessness of consumerist culture. Such disillusionment lay behind the protests of students and workers in France in May 1968. Movements such as these served the prophetic function of culture criticism but they could not provide solutions or alternatives in terms of a more humane society and greater justice for people, and often led to bitter disappointment and cynicism.

The *economic gap between the rich and the poor* widened further, despite all the well-meant development projects. The gap grew not only between the North and the South but also within both Northern and Southern societies. Power struggles and the emphasis on economic gain led to a loss of respect for human life and for the creation as a whole. This was shown by the ruthless exploitation of indigenous people and their land by multinational corporations. In Western societies there was growing licentiousness. The Sharpeville massacre of 1960 brought home to the world the harsh, dehumanizing nature of white minority rule in South Africa. The genocide in Biafra showed the inhuman face of nationalism in Africa and elsewhere. The 1960s were marked by fanaticism and terrorism, and the assassination of outstanding personalities like John Kennedy and Martin Luther King. The struggle against such destructive tendencies also grew in an organized way as, for instance, through the work of

Amnesty International, which exposed widespread torture in the East, West and South.

Out of this world, increasing numbers of participants from all continents came to Bossey. Their hopes and angers, aspirations and fears had to be taken up in its work in the light of the gospel and the community of the worldwide church. In a small way this was reflected in the Bossey team and programme.

The staff team under Wolf

Bossey could no longer work with just two resident members of the teaching staff or just one interpreter. A larger staff was needed to cope with the expanding work (see appendix B). From 1956 onwards Bossey had a teaching staff of three, then four, and plans were afoot to have a fifth member. A full-time librarian was needed for the expanding library and two, at times three, interpreters now ensured simultaneous translation for English, French and German. The office and the house staff also had to be strengthened.

The main responsibility for the programme lay with the board and the members of the teaching staff. The actual running and the life of the Institute depended much on others who really became *the "pillars" of Bossey*. Three of them are singled out here because of their long-term service, the excellence of their work and their total commitment to the vocation of the Institute.

— Simone Mathil worked for many years as the head of the office, and only she would be able tell us what it meant, year after year, to have a group of some fifty students for the Graduate School from all parts of the world, and to attend to all the details of entry visas, travel arrangements and university accreditation.

— Herman de Graaf served the Institute for almost twenty years as accountant, and for many participants also as a lay pastor. He could tell us about the problems that ensue when a student from overseas has an accident at Bossey, insured for care in Switzerland but not for after-care in his home country.

— Margret Koch, the librarian, worked for 27 years for the Institute. Directors, doctoral students and participants of the Graduate Schools would hardly have been able to finish their lectures, dissertations and term papers in time without her help. With her knowledge in the field of liturgy and her special concern for Orthodox and Catholic participants, her service went far beyond the library.

The difficulties which the pioneers had experienced in their work remained as *continuing dilemmas for the teaching staff*. In the directors' reports and the minutes of the board the same questions recur periodically. How can serious preparation be combined with ongoing teaching of very diverse subjects? How does one remain in touch with the churches and societies in various countries while being fully present and available at the Institute? How can one initiate new work, gathering ever new groups, and at the same time find the time to keep in contact with former participants and attend to all the necessary follow-up? In cooperating with the WCC headquarters staff, how does one preserve a certain freedom and distance that Bossey's own creative work requires? All proposed division of work in Bossey itself proved difficult in practice because the tasks were closely inter-related and interdependent. All members of the faculty thus remained involved in the Graduate School. Responsibility for organizing and carrying through a summer course or a frontier conference was by common agreement assigned to one or another member of the faculty.

From 1955 to 1966 *Hans-Heinrich Wolf* gave leadership to the team. He was a German Lutheran professor of systematic theology who had been deeply influenced by the church struggle against the Nazi ideology. Before coming to Bossey he taught at the theological school of Bethel, on the same campus with the Bodelschwingh institutions for physically and mentally handicapped persons. Theology was done there in the context of daily human suffering, and it received a pastoral dimension often lacking in purely academic settings. A tall, tense man, Wolf directed Bossey and its team in a strict way, assuming fully the task of leadership. Some felt he was too authoritarian. Those who came to know him more personally respected him as a person of complete integrity and a man of spiritual authority. He made great demands first of all on himself, but also on his colleagues. When exploring a subject together with fellow theologians, Jewish thinkers, artists or nuclear physicists, theology never remained for him just a matter of the mind. It passed, so to say, through his whole body and at times he became physically ill after such existential encounters. He had also great aesthetic sensitivity. After leaving Bossey, Wolf became professor of ecumenics at Bochum University in Germany.

Wolf's major contribution was the further development of the Graduate School which, after the first three experimental years, had

acquired an established format. Under his direction the first doctorates in ecumenical studies were completed. Wolf had also a
passion for building. It was due to his persistent efforts to secure
special grants from Germany that the lecture hall and the library
were built. Added in the chapel during his time were the communion
table, the large wooden cross, the wall with the glass mosaic. After
much consultation Frère Marc of the Taizé community created this
mosaic which was paid for mainly by Asian women through the
Movement of the Least Coin. Churches in East Germany donated
and installed the organ.

The first member of the new teaching team was *Robert S. Paul*, a
church historian and minister of the Congregational Church of Great
Britain and Wales, who worked at Bossey for four year from 1954. He
was a local parish minister, and on the basis of this experience had
much to contribute to the programme of the Institute where courses for
theological students and ministers were gaining in importance. Paul
also started the series of meetings with professors of different theological disciplines. The first of these brought together church historians
who examined how church history could be taught within an ecumenical perspective. After his time in Bossey, Paul taught at Hartford
Seminary in the USA.

When in 1956 a third member of the teaching staff could be
appointed, *Charles C. West* was invited. He was a teacher of social
ethics, from the Presbyterian Church in the USA, and he served
Bossey for five years. He had worked in the midst of a revolutionary
situation as a lecturer and student chaplain in China until he was
caught between the withdrawing nationalist troops and the advancing
communist army. After this Chinese exposure, West worked first in
Germany, with the Gossner Mission, among secularized industrial
workers and for the WCC's reconstruction department in Berlin, then
in the USA training missionaries. With this rich experience West
initiated in Bossey a new reflection on secularization. He helped many
to rethink mission for a revolutionary world and to face the challenge
of Marxism. After Bossey, West became a professor at Princeton
Theological Seminary.

A young Greek Orthodox lay theologian, *Nikos Nissiotis*, joined
the teaching staff in 1958. He had served as a tutor for the fourth
Graduate School. Visser 't Hooft saw him as one who might help the
World Council and Bossey in interpreting Orthodox faith for the

modern world. His contributions were substantial and of great significance, as we shall see later.

A fourth resident member, *Henry F. Makulu*, joined the team in 1960. A layman from the United Church in Zambia (then Northern Rhodesia), he was the first African on the Bossey faculty. With his experience in social work and civil service he was for four years mainly involved in lay courses and conferences on social and industrial questions. From Bossey Makulu went to the lay training centre in Mindolo, and became an adviser of president Kaunda.

When West returned to the USA in 1961, *Hans-Ruedi Weber* took over as associate director, serving Bossey for ten years. A Swiss Reformed theologian, he was a disciple of both Kraemer and Suzanne de Diétrich. He had worked as theological teacher on the islands of Celebes and Java in Indonesia and, after the Evanston assembly, had become the successor of H.-H. Walz in the WCC's department on the laity. In the Institute's programme he was much involved in questions on the ministry of the laity, the rethinking of missions and participatory ways of Bible studies. He was particularly interested in the frontier conferences, especially those in relation to life sciences, industry and futurology. His assignment, after Bossey, was with the biblical studies secretariat at the World Council.

The first Asian on the faculty joined in 1964, the Indian *Samuel L. Parmar*. This professor of economics taught at Bossey on a three-year leave of absence from the state university of Allahabad. Later he served the Institute as a board member. He helped many to see realistically how national and international economics work. He uncovered the naiveté of much thinking and planning with regard to "economic development". As critical of the oppressive forces in his own country as he was of Western economic exploitation, he used no simplifying slogans, but pointed to the need to work for fundamental structural changes in the societies both of affluence and of poverty. What impressed those who worked with him most was the deep Christian faith of this economist. For Westerners he became a source of quiet and strength; he taught them to walk and work in harmony with nature, with a long-term perspective and a holy patience — as the following story illustrates.

We were waiting for Sam. Every Monday the teaching staff and those responsible for running the house gathered after lunch in the director's office. Together we planned the week ahead. Parmar had only recently joined our team but we had already come to respect and love him and his family. We knew that he was on the campus, and some of us Westerners began to become impatient. Then we saw the door opening very slowly and Sam standing there, silent and solemn. "Now something terrible has happened to me," he finally said, still not moving towards the empty chair. "Leaving home I knew I would be late for the meeting. So I began to hurry as you people usually do. Then I suddenly stopped hurrying, stood still and realized how much even during these first weeks here I was in danger of losing my identity and inheritance. So I came very slowly, step by step."

The staff team with Nissiotis

There was a smooth change-over of leadership when, in 1966, Wolf left and Nissiotis became the third director of the Institute. He had already worked eight years at Bossey, and his colleagues and the house staff knew him well. Programmes were not interrupted, and could develop in the way they had grown since 1955. What changed was the leadership style, from a strict German pattern to a more Mediterranean geniality.

The intellectual gifts and qualifications which Nissiotis brought to Bossey were remarkable. He had grown up in the family of an Orthodox priest in Athens and his father, the saintly Fr Angelos, had become the leader of a lay movement which worked for the renewal of church life in Greece. Nissiotis had been much involved in the Greek Student Christian Movement. He studied philosophy, theology, psychology and sociology in Athens, Zurich (under Emil Brunner and Carl-Gustav Jung), Basel (under Karl Barth and Karl Jaspers) and at the Catholic faculty in Louvain. He was also a keen sportsman and later played a leading role in the Olympic movement. As one of the first Orthodox theologians working full-time on the World Council staff Nissiotis had to take on many tasks: WCC observer at the Second Vatican Council, guest lectureships and, from 1968 onwards, besides being director of Bossey, also to serve as associate general secretary of the Council. He knew how to develop a team and a friendly atmosphere, and how to delegate tasks. What he did not like was to make decisions on delicate and controversial issues, and he delegated these too to his colleagues!

The *main contribution of Nissiotis* was his stimulating way of teaching. He liked honest debates, could listen to opinions different from his own and then, with great competence, enter into dialogue without putting down less knowledgeable partners. Rooted in his Orthodox faith he became passionately involved with Protestant and Roman Catholic thinkers, with existentialist philosophers and scientists, in the search for truth with regard to questions posed by the world. Through his teaching in the Orthodox seminars at Bossey he initiated many into Orthodox ways of theological thinking and to the understanding of icons.

A Pakistani political scientist, *Anwar Barkat* joined the teaching team in 1967 after Parmar returned to India. Coming from a situation where Christians form a small minority among militant Muslims and from a society marked by explosive power politics, Barkat was much involved both at the Institute and the WCC headquarters with studies on international affairs. In less than three years he was called back to Pakistan to take over as principal in a Christian college.

Meanwhile, a young American Methodist and New Testament scholar, *Joseph C. Weber*, had in 1966 joined the staff. He had excellent contacts with theological students and also helped in pioneering meetings with conservative Evangelicals who were often critical of World Council policies. After three years at Bossey he went back to the US to continue teaching New Testament at several theological schools in the USA.

Another young theologian took his place for a three year term, the Anglican social ethicist *Michael Keeling* from Great Britain. In the late 1960s, with the strong student protests in many places, the presence of young members on the teaching staff was a great asset. Keeling helped much with specialized conferences and was responsible, among others, for a meeting with people in industry.

There were *no women on the teaching staff* during the 1955-70 period. On the Bossey board too women formed only a small minority, though a remarkable woman, the British educationalist Kathleen Bliss, was its moderator between the WCC assemblies in Evanston and New Delhi. In the early years the presence of Suzanne de Diétrich had shown how important the special sensitivity and intuition of a woman can be for the planning and holding of meetings in a place like Bossey. Women guest lecturers and tutors made substantial contributions, though it was only in 1986 that a woman once again became a member of the resident teaching team.

Nevertheless, during that period the contribution of women was considerable, and covered many areas of life at Bossey. They were the leaders in the house, the office and the library. The difficult and important work of simultaneous interpretation was carried out mainly by highly qualified women. Among those who served the Institute as interpreters for many years were Margaret Pater, Dorli Kimmel and Bärbel Fischer. After Renée Sturm, the key hospitality post was held first by Renée Béguin and then by Eva-Maria Schneck, two "châtelaines" whom many remember with deep thankfulness.

A time of growth

The years from 1955 to 1970 were a period of growth, not only for Bossey but for the whole ecumenical movement. A mood of expectancy prevailed. At the WCC assembly in New Delhi in 1961 the Orthodox churches of East Europe joined its membership and the International Missionary Council merged with the World Council. In a divided world, it seemed the covenanting churches could become a real force of healing and change, all the more so now that the Second Vatican Council from 1962 to 1965 had raised great hopes. Could Christian churches finally be united? Were the courageous stances of the Latin American bishops conference in Medellín (1968) an indication of things to come? Christians felt confident that they could discern the signs of the times. With their global vision of humanity and creation they hoped to be able to lead the nations on the way to peace and justice. This mood expressed itself strongly in the world conference on Church and Society in Geneva in 1966 and it was reflected in the message of the assembly at Uppsala in 1968.

A steady growth also marked the life and work of Bossey. The main elements of the Institute's programme were now set. In addition to the Graduate School semester each year, the three main ecumenical education summer courses were held for theological students, pastors/priests/missionaries, and lay people. The Berlin courses continued until the early 1970s. Similar extension work was attempted twice in Finland and once in the Middle East. With the presence of an Orthodox theologian on the teaching team, an annual two-week Orthodox seminar was added to these from 1959. After a consultation on education within the armed forces, for several years courses were also offered for army chaplains. And the interdisciplinary frontier conferences continued, with the time-consuming preparatory work they demanded, as well as conferences on special issues of church life.

During the period under consideration the number of participants increased. A statistical survey for the 1946 to 1959 period shows that nearly ten thousand people attended Bossey meetings, coming from all major Christian confessions and all regions of the world except the Pacific islands. Roman Catholics still formed only a small minority. Because of the iron curtain fewer people now came from Eastern Europe. The number of Asians and Africans had gone up, but Latin Americans remained under-represented, mainly because Spanish never became an official language at Bossey. Around 1970 it was sometimes difficult to get good European representation. A survey of participants for that year lists 776 persons and indicates that all the major courses had between 45 and 55 participants. The percentage of Orthodox and Roman Catholics had become substantially higher than in 1959, and there were now also a few participants from the Soviet Union.

With such a steady rise in the number of participants, a well-equipped *lecture hall and library* were needed, for which extra-budgetary funds had to be found. The Council's finance committee rejected the proposal of the board to get money for the new buildings by selling Petit Bossey. To provide more rooms the top floor of that mansion was redone. Only when substantial grants from Germany and a gift from the canton of Geneva were received could the building of the present lecture hall and library begin.

With the growth of work, increase in the number of participants and the provision of new amenities, inevitably Bossey had to have a *bigger budget*. Since 1954 the Institute had received annually for its working budget a sum of US$60-65,000 out of the general budget of the World Council. After the assemblies in 1961 and 1968 this working budget had been increased. But still there was never suffi-cient money for scholarships. Nor could all the plans for improving the existing amenities and putting up more lodgings for the staff be carried out. Nevertheless, during that period finance did not threaten the survival of Bossey. The financial worries of the board and the staff were rather over securing new funds for further growth.

In the circumstances one would have expected Bossey to be given a more important place in the World Council. This did not happen. During the period *Bossey was actually losing visibility*. In the minutes of the WCC central committees and the reports of the assemblies less and less attention and space were given to the work of the Institute. This was mainly due to the fact that in the same period the whole work of the Council had expanded. In several regions institutions were coming up to promote, on a national or regional level, ecumenical education and study. Their work was in some respects similar to what was being done at Bossey. The Institute had indeed functioned as a "seminary", a place of sowing. Certain pioneering initiatives were thus beginning to bear fruit. They were taken up and developed by newly created departments of the World Council or by regional centres. This was the case with regard to the concern over the ministry of the laity in the world. It was true also of subjects in the realm of social ethics, health services, education and intercultural and inter-religious dialogue.

Even before 1970 *critical questions* were asked about Bossey, about its ability to continue pioneering work, and not only by outsiders and WCC headquarters staff. The questions were also in the minds of the Bossey staff, and the board discussed them repeatedly. Kathleen Bliss, its moderator, had worked with J.H. Oldham and shared his concern for maintaining high standards in ecumenical studies and action. Walter Mülder, the board's moderator from 1961, had often reflected on the need for and the dangers of the process of institutionalization, thus helping the staff to look critically at their own work. Board members, like the Dutch economist Harry M. de Lange, forcefully reminded the staff and the board of the primary church-world function of Bossey, its specific vocation to work on frontier issues. The Graduate School board insisted on higher academic standards and serious theological work. But what kind of theological work — asked the Asian and African members of the two boards? Did the link with Geneva university mean that continental European ways of doing theology should be normative for shaping the programme and the requirements for an ecumenical diploma or doctorate?

Since 1954 Bossey had become part of the World Council's Division of Ecumenical Action, though it still continued to work with all the other programme divisions. Often members of the Council's governing bodies and of the headquarters staff saw the Institute as another "programme" without sufficiently recognizing the different work conditions and styles of a resident learning fellowship and an educational institution. This led to tensions. In 1971, when the

Council's structure was reviewed, the Institute came once again under the direct supervision of the General Secretariat.

The experiment of the Graduate School

No semester of the Graduate School has been the same as any other. The experiment continued without ever finding a definitive schedule and way of learning which could be safely repeated for the next semester. Year after year the directors tried to make changes, responding to criticism and to suggestions received from past students and the board. Yet with each new group, new theme and time, such changes often became the most seriously contended element. Nevertheless, as the number of students grew from 25 to over 50, most of them theologically trained persons, some basic experiences stood out, and gradually certain patterns emerged, some of which have continued to mark the life of Bossey.

At the beginning of each semester everybody feels a stranger. This initial experience of alienation is immediately felt in the matter of language. Most participants must communicate with others in what for them is a foreign language. When English is spoken, which is most often the case, even the British find it difficult to understand the strange accents and the broken English from all over the world. They soon make the disconcerting discovery that their perfect English is in fact less easily understood than the outlandish versions of the language. Even with the help of excellent interpreters it is a strain and tiring to understand and make oneself understood through simultaneous interpretation. To have to write a term paper in one's second or third language can become a torture. Such language difficulties healthily check superficial theological rhetoric, and force both teachers and participants to think and speak more clearly and at a more fundamental level. But language is only one among many other alienating factors at the start of each Graduate School. Even resident staff members sometimes feel like strangers, and have to make an effort to become part of the microcosmic group that has taken over the house.

In the period from 1955 to 1970 little conscious sensitivity training or methodological *community building* was attempted. The learning and worshipping fellowship had to grow through trial and error. For the first week-end an outing was normally planned, walking to the abbey of Bonmont or making an excursion in the Jura mountains. For several years a football match (European style) took place that week-end: a student team against a team of the staff. Coached by Nissiotis, the staff team did not always lose and, together with other sports events, the match helped to create community. After the first few weeks a student committee was elected which discussed and decided, together with the staff, community problems and events. In almost every group members with special pastoral gifts were gradually discovered, and they supported participants who were feeling lonely or left out, and helped the fellowship to grow. The appointment of a chaplain for the Graduate School was discussed several times, but chaplaincy work for such a multilingual and diverse group goes beyond the gifts of just one person.

A member of the 13th semester wrote twenty years later that for him the outstanding experience of the Graduate School had been "a combination of debates, laughter and *worship* — debates in the lecture hall, laughter in the dining hall and worship in the chapel". This sums up the experience of many. An attempt is indeed made at Bossey to root both study and community life in worship. Yet worship often becomes the most difficult part of the total programme. In the period under consideration there still were daily morning prayers, the noon intercessions led by the staff and an evening prayer. The programme provided for a eucharistic service for the whole community twice a month. Quite a few Protestants felt that all this was a little too much and too heavy, and in the weeks before the deadline for term papers the number of worshippers dwindled. Nevertheless, many learned at Bossey the value of regular daily worship. The elected worship committee often proceeded in the following way: one confessional group would be responsible for conducting either morning or evening services for two weeks. All participants thus learned to sing typical liturgical responses and hymns of that confession. Towards the end of the fortnight there would be a lecture and discussion on the liturgical heritage of that confessional family, and on Sunday communion according to that tradition was celebrated. All students were expected to attend, though they could not all take part in the eucharist. Year after year the Graduate School thus painfully experienced the scandal of division. There were times when community life reached such a depth, especially when hurts and reconciliation had been experienced, that despite ecclesiastical discipline and the prevailing practice of the World Council eucharistic sharing did take place.

The semester was divided into *three periods*, and at the end of each a term paper had to be submitted. These papers replaced the earlier exams, and sometimes the papers were written and presented corporately by seminar groups. During the relatively short first period an experienced ecumenical leader, most often Visser 't Hooft, lectured on the history of the ecumenical movement, and confessional studies were introduced. During the long second period the main theme was dealt with through lectures and seminars. The third period usually concentrated on the implications of the main theme for the life and mission of the church, and on seminars introducing current WCC work.

In the 1950s there was still strong emphasis on *confessional studies*. During each semester two confessional families were introduced, but later only one. Towards the end of the 1960s the interest for such confessional studies clearly declined. It would be wrong, however, to underestimate the continuing influence of different confessional heritages. In almost every Graduate School the following development could be observed: at the beginning participants were excited to meet fellow Christians from other cultures and confessions. Then came for many a period of self-discovery and self-defence: Lutherans became more Lutheran, Anglicans more Anglican and Orthodox more Orthodox. Only gradually a third stage was reached when participants became ready to learn from other confessional heritages, to discover together a common tradition and to transcend confessional barriers in search of a fuller truth. Kraemer had observed that confronting participants with a study of Orthodoxy is one of the best ways to realize both the depth and difficulty of the ecumenical movement. In the period under consideration the days after the Christmas break were usually devoted to an introduction to Orthodox worship, always linked to attendance at the epiphany service in an Orthodox church in Geneva. Such Orthodox study days continued even after other confessional studies tended to disappear.

The main *themes of the Graduate Schools* reflect the major agenda points of the world, the churches and the World Council (appendix A). During the first years several themes from the areas of Church and Society, Faith and Order, and Mission and Evangelism were taken up. Gradually studies were centred on just one theme which was explored biblically, systematically and with a strong emphasis on discovering its practical implications for the churches' vocation in the world. For the teaching staff these themes were of first importance, but not necessarily for the students. Former participants do not always remember the theme, but they rarely forget the experience of living, worshipping and studying together in a fellowship of people with many confessional and cultural backgrounds.

For studying these themes *various ways of learning and teaching* were followed. In the 1950s lectures were the main medium, followed by plenary discussions. For dealing with the theme outstanding theologians from various confessions and many parts of the world, specialists in related academic disciplines and often also secular humanists and representatives of other faiths, would be invited. Gradually more emphasis was laid on work in seminar groups and tutorials. Theme visits were also organized. When studying the relation between the church and the Jewish people in the 13th semester participants visited Jewish institutions and attended synagogue worship. A year later when the theme was on the church in a technocratic world, participants visited a machine factory, a large cooperative enterprise and a central hospital. Each year the schedule included a week-end visit to Swiss local parishes, and often also a visit to the Taizé community in France. During several semesters students went to Basel for a seminar with Karl Barth.

Only a few Graduate School students used Bossey's link with Geneva university for continuing ecumenical research with a view to securing an *ecumenical diploma or an ecumenical doctorate*. During the semester community activities were so time-consuming and the themes explored so vast that only very disciplined participants could start work on their own research project. The first two diplomas were granted in 1955. The requirements for the doctoral programme were set so high, especially with regard to languages, that only a few attempted to get this degree and even fewer actually had their dissertation accepted. In the 1955-71 period seven ecumenical doctorates were granted, but since then only two more have completed their research (see list at the end of appendix C). Several others started research at Bossey, but presented their dissertation in other universities and not in Geneva.

In 1963 the board of the Graduate School had a long discussion on the future of ecumenical research, on the basis of a paper prepared by Edmund Schlink. A year later the Faith and Order department made a concrete proposal for establishing an *Ecumenical Research Institute* in

relation to Bossey and its Graduate School. The plan was to convert
the barn at Petit Bossey for the use of three permanent research
fellows and visiting researchers. This proposal has been discussed
several times since but due to lack of funds it could not be implemented.

With financial help from the WCC Inter-Church Aid Department,
a *field-work programme* was started in 1962 for up to 15 Graduate
School participants. They were placed for three months in critical
frontier situations, for instance with industrial mission teams in
Germany or Great Britain, in local parish work with a confession other
than their own, in lay training centres, or as trainees in a World
Council department. Occasionally students were sent beyond Europe,
to Lebanon, Algeria or a kibbutz in Israel. After field-work they came
back to Bossey for a week's evaluation. Those who went through this
experience, both students and staff, will always remember that final
week of deep conversations, prayer and friendship.

What remains best remembered are the *intercultural encounters*.
For participants of the Graduate School each continent and several of
its countries and cultures become a group of faces, persons who are
often friends. Conscious or unconscious cultural and racial prejudices
are discovered and, alas, not always overcome. During the 1950s and
1960s this was most dramatically the case for the white, coloured and
black students coming from South Africa. Many a Graduate School
had to live through the pains and healing processes of that situation. In
other semesters the living together of people coming from cultures of
poverty and cultures of material abundance proved difficult. Participants from the USA often became victims of prejudice because of
their country's affluence and power politics. Gradually also the
challenge to chauvinist masculine ways of behaviour began to play a
role in the intercultural growing processes. Since the late 1950s
cultural week-ends have become an important part of the programme.
Every second week one continental or regional group of participants
presents the socio-political, cultural and ecclesiastical situation from
which they come. This is complemented by a cultural evening, with
music, humour and dance, often ending with a typical meal cooked
together by students and the kitchen staff.

What started simply as a social event increasingly turned into the
discovery of *intercultural theology*. Participants grew sensitive to
culturally conditioned ways of thinking. The most heated theological

debates often arose not due to the different confessional heritages but because of various ways of theologizing in different cultures. For Westerners it was a healthy but traumatic experience to discover that their way of doing theology is not *the* normative way. For many Africans and Asians it became a new and exciting experience to learn in the transcultural encounters at Bossey to think theologically as Africans and Asians.

At the frontier of church and world

Speaking about the Bossey conferences and consultations Wolf said in his first report to the WCC central committee in 1956:

> The purpose of these is to explore areas on the frontier between the church and the world where new thinking and action is urgently needed. They are the most expensive of all Bossey activities in terms both of staff time and money, but also they are the basic reason for the existence of the Ecumenical Institute.

Ten years later, Wolf asked critically in his last oral report to the board: "Did we really do frontier work? In a way, yes, at least in our planning." He mentioned some of the frontier issues that had been dealt with, but pointed to the fact that often it was the theologian who found it most difficult to enter into a common search with specialists of other disciplines. Wolf then recalled Oldham's method, commending it for Bossey. Oldham started with a few experts, which led to a small consultation; only then would he prepare a conference with broader participation. If one surveys the many complex frontier issues taken up during the 1955-70 period, it becomes evident that Wolf's critical questioning was fully justified, and only little could be done in the same thorough way Oldham had shown.

Compared with the period of the pioneers, there was now a *shift from professional to interdisciplinary meetings*. Occasionally, conferences were called for people in the medical and nursing professions, for educators, architects, social workers and lawyers, but the emphasis now was on important questions of the day, to address which a variety of specialists from different fields of knowledge were invited. Here we mention only the major series of such conferences (see reports in appendix C).

Basic reflection had to continue on *the present world and history* within which Christians are called to witness. This meant that studies on the process of secularization, begun at the world conferences of Oxford and Jerusalem before the war, had to continue. Under Kraemer's leadership, the Bossey meeting on the meaning of history had already taken up further reflection on secularization as a force, atmosphere and attitude pervading modern life. It was generally defined as "the withdrawal of areas of thought and life from religious — and finally also from metaphysical — control, and the attempt to understand and live in these areas in the terms which they alone offer". While this process can have a liberating effect, it also fragments and relativizes human life and knowledge. What then is truth? And where are the criteria for responsible action in such a world? Meetings of philosophers and theologians organized by Wolf discussed these questions.

The interdisciplinary consultation in 1959 on *the meaning of the secular* was a seminal event leading to further reflection. It was prepared by West in collaboration with the World Student Christian Federation. Participants came mainly from the Western world, with some influential persons from Asia and Eastern Europe, both Christians and secular humanists. Many university faculties were represented. The starting point was the definition given above, but already when discussing the historical background of secularization there surfaced a fundamental difference. Is this process conceivable only within a Greek and Christian context, proceeding from the European middle ages via the time of Enlightenment to the modern West and then increasingly to all continents? Or can, for instance, the Buddhist revolt of the 5th century BC against the Brahmin priestly caste be considered as marking the beginning of a similar secularization process? And what about modern China? What is the relation between Confucianism and the growing Maoist ideology which may produce in China secular attitudes similar to the Western? Equally fundamental differences also emerged when discussing the values and dangers of the secularization process and its expected outcome.

In the Bossey frontier conferences of the 1960s the distinction between *secularization and secularism* received increasing emphasis. Even at the 1959 consultation, Dietrich Bonhoeffer's thoughts about humanity as mature in its secularity and about the non-religious interpretation of theological concepts had played an important role. Then A.Th. van Leeuwen's study on *Christianity in World History* (1964) strongly influenced Bossey conferences. In it the processes of secularization are seen in the first place as a liberating development which can be observed already in the Old and New Testament challenge to the sacralization of the secular. However, these processes must be disciplined lest they should become a closed ideology of secularism. Such reflections led to a theological consultation on the lordship of Christ and his presence in the world. Many summer courses examined the Christian vocation in the light of these insights.

The last large conference in this more general interdisciplinary reflection dealt, in 1969, with the theme: *Man, the steward of power.* Nissiotis, the main organizer of the meeting, wrote that its aim was to face the fact that

> the progress of modern sciences accumulates in the hands of man an ever-growing power to transform society, contributing thus to a rapid rise in the standard of living in general. This development raises, first, the question of whether man himself is affected by this increase in his capacity to code and to control the enormous possibilities that modern science puts into his hands and, second, of whether these sciences cause such radical transformations that they affect man's self-understanding and his responsibility as a social being.

The conference started with a confrontation between theoreticians and engineers of the computer sciences to which respectively a biologist, a psychiatrist, a nuclear physicist and a sociologist responded. This in turn led to philosophical, biblical and systematic theological comments and to interdisciplinary group work.

Frontier issues

A first major series of more specialized frontier conferences concentrated on *the East-West tension and the struggle for peace.* Under Wolf's leadership gatherings of scientists (especially in physics) and theologians had already taken up the old question of the relationship between science and faith. In the context of the nuclear arms race this reflection received a new urgency. What is the Christian responsibility in the realm of the application of discoveries in nuclear physics? Three meetings of politicians, lawyers and theologians explored the questions: What is the role of responsible political decision-making in the critical cold-war situation? How can Christians help in the search for an international ethos? What are alternatives to conflict in the quest for peace?

The major contribution of Bossey towards *East-West reconciliation* was a series of conferences prepared by Nissiotis. The first meeting introduced key people from the West to East European culture and church life in order to prepare them for encounters with Christians from there. The series continued with conferences on Eastern and Western spirituality, on God's reconciling work among the nations, and finally a meeting on reconciliation and international justice. Nissiotis commented on an important shift in interest:

> The spectre of cold war lent an urgency to these deliberations. But the last conference moved beyond this frame of reference and concentrated on issues emerging from the so-called "North-South tension", the strains in relations between "rich" and "poor" or "developed" and "developing" nations. The Ecumenical Institute is perhaps one of the most appropriate places for a discussion of this kind, and it may well be one of the main tasks of present-day ecumenism to break through this division into political, cultural and theological blocs which chain the minds of some people today.

Another series of specialized conferences dealt with the frontier between *churches and the industrial/economic world*. Questions of work and vocation, especially in the industrial world and, to a lesser degree, in farming, had from the beginning been present on Bossey's agenda. Only seldom could factory workers and rural labourers participate in such interdisciplinary conferences. Workers were mainly represented by people and action groups serving among migrant labourers, by trade union leaders, industrial chaplains and leaders of farming organizations. This clearly is one of the weaknesses of an international venue for such encounters, and it has to be recognized as one of Bossey's built-in limitations.

This early Bossey concern for questions regarding *decision-making and leadership* in industry and economy was pursued in the 1960s through several meetings at the Institute, often organized together with the WCC departments on Church and Society and on the Laity. Wolf was responsible for a conference on questions related to the developing European Common Market, calling together industrialists and church leaders. The author of this story had a great deal to do with other gatherings in this series. One of them was an attempt to explore the theme of a Christian attitude to money. It started with a survey of varying attitudes to material wealth in different cultures and confessions. This led to an examination of how economic structures influence life, including the life of churches. On the basis of these two enquiries the meeting worked towards an understanding of what Christian ethics teaches about financial involvement and responsibility. Another meeting looked at the relationship between human engineering and Christian growth. Industrial personnel managers and both Christian and secular specialists involved in adult education gathered together to explore the possibilities and dangers of influencing personal and group attitudes and beliefs with methods learned in the behavioural sciences. The aim was to discover ways of influencing change that are neither authoritarian nor manipulative but develop the gifts and possibilities of persons and groups.

In this frontier area of industrial decision-making, perhaps the most interesting conference was the one that dealt with *industrial democracy in a technocratic age*. Business managers, trade union leaders, government officials, economists and Christian, Marxist and secular students of social ethics came together to assess critically recent attempts to let workers participate in the decision-making processes, and also to share in the profits. After looking at the future of the industrial society, participants discussed the merits and dangers of such experiments in industrial democracy in western Germany and Yugoslavia. The background paper for the conference said: "The realization of industrial democracy must not be seen as a better care for employees. It is not part of the welfare state. Industrial democracy aims at changing the existing power structures on all levels." Obviously not all agreed with such a radical position and there were great tensions in the group.

It is in groups where strong present-day political and socio-economic convictions come into conflict that *Bible study at the frontier* becomes most meaningful. It is then rewarding to listen together to biblical witnesses from another time and socio-cultural context that address similar basic human predicaments. Whether these biblical texts are examined simply as important literary and historical documents or accepted with full canonical authority, they can function as a third voice in the dialogue. This was the case at the industrial democracy conference. Although about one-third of the participants were not Christians, the meeting included Bible studies, exploring texts on human vocation, on prophetic protest, on legislation and sacrifice. Some of the Marxist and secular humanist participants showed a keener interest for such studies than the Christians!

A further series of interdisciplinary conferences dealt with *issues at the frontier between body and mind*. From its origin, Bossey had a special interest in convening meetings with medical doctors, nursing personnel and people involved in pastoral ministry among the sick and the suffering. In the 1960s great interest had developed not only for studying the relationship between a person's body and mind (psychosomatic illnesses) but also the relationship between the body of society and mental/physical illness or health of individuals (socio-pathology).

A conference on *our common mental illness and health* thus brought together psychiatrists, psychologists, chaplains in mental hospitals and theologians, among them major proponents of socio-pathology and representatives of therapeutic communities in several regions. Three questions were explored:

> How far is it true to say that mentally and physically ill people suffer vicariously for the whole society, and what is the relevance of the biblical message about vicarious suffering in this respect? To what extent can one say that illness is caused by transpersonal powers and what has the biblical message about Christ's victory over satanic powers to say about this question? What is the role of therapeutic communities, and to what extent can the church as we see it in the New Testament and as it exists today be such a healing community?

There was great interest in this meeting and, in some cases unannounced, more participants came than could be accommodated. This created much tension among the house staff and in the kitchen. The socio-pathologists straight away began to analyze the resident community of Bossey as a socio-pathological case! It was not easy to host and direct such a large interdisciplinary encounter while being treated as a patient. At the end of the meeting several of the resident staff, including the author who had major responsibility for this series of conferences, were on the brink of mental breakdown. Nevertheless, that encounter too became for many a seminal event.

The discovery of the genetic code, organ transplants and new psycho-pharmaceutical medicaments and drugs led to a conference on *experiments with human beings*. Biologists, biochemists, pharmacologists, professors of medicine and theologians met to discuss the possibilities, dangers and limits of biomedical experimentation, necessary for testing new medicaments and for healing certain illnesses. An International Code of Medical Ethics had been accepted by the World Medical Association, but with the rapid development of science and research the rules of the Helsinki declaration on human experimentation needed to be reformulated. Many researchers worked in a risky ethical and legal no-man's-land. One purpose of the conference was to initiate the necessary revision of the declaration. The report was submitted to medical associations and the World Health Organisation.

Still another conference with representatives mainly of medical sciences and theologians dealt with the *wisdom of the body*. After the main inputs by a physiologist, an anthropologist, a biblical exegete and a philosopher, the conference explored what we can learn from the wisdom of the body, how the body functions as a medium of communication and what distinguishes human beings from animals. A few physiotherapists, TV and drama producers were also present, and they helped to give the theoretical discussions some flesh and blood. An evening performance through the medium of mime helped the participants to discover the rich possibilities of bodily expressions. Several members of that conference participated in a small consultation immediately following it on sports in a Christian perspective. Together with a group of sports physicians and sports teachers, they critically examined what Christians have to learn from and contribute to the growing phenomenon of popular sports. What were the prophetic warnings that high performance sports and the commercial and political exploitation of sports events called for? The conclusions of this consultation were fed into the world scientific congress on sports preceding the Olympic Games in Munich.

Issues of church life

The reflection on the process of secularization and the various frontier conferences had a strong influence also on the Graduate Schools and summer courses which dealt with issues of church life. *Christian presence in the world* became an over-arching general theme of the whole 1955-70 period. Several meetings dealt with questions concerning the life-style needed for such a presence, often collaborating with studies of the Council's department on the laity. Could Christian presence be best described as a "holy worldliness"? When was the "incognito" of believers necessary and when was a bold prophetic stance and an outspoken testimony called for? How could the double conversion, that from the world and that to the world, be held together? How could Christians deal with the challenge of social evils?

In this connection several Bossey meetings examined the needed renewal of *structures of church life*. How do Christian communities relate to sociological communities? Long after the Constantinian era and in a world that has little to do with Christendom, almost everywhere Christians have become a minority. This led to a theological reflection on the future of the world and the churches, especially the diaspora situation of Christians. Both the annual extension courses in Berlin with Christians from Eastern Europe and the presence of first an African and then two Asian staff members put this question on the Bossey agenda. A good collaboration was established between the Institute and two ongoing World Council studies, one on rapid social change and the other on the missionary structure of the congregation. The 9th, 12th, 14th, 16th and 18th Graduate Schools concentrated on such issues.

The reflections on the missionary presence of the churches in the world led to a few meetings with those who are often called *conservative evangelicals* with their critical stance with regard to the Council's thinking on mission and the Council's ways of biblical interpretation. These encounters between equal numbers of "evangelical" and "ecumenical" participants led to honest and fruitful contacts and mutual correction. There was at Bossey a growing interest in establishing more contacts with Pentecostals, and some outstanding Pentecostal leaders were invited as speakers and resource persons. In the context of the fast-growing movements of conservative evangelicals and Pentecostals Bossey devoted a summer course to God's mission and church growth, critically examining missionary theories and strategies which measure the success or failure of witness to Christ mainly in terms of numerical church growth.

The concern for an authentic Christian presence in the world and the critical situation in the Near East led to much reflection on *Jewish thinking and presence*. Outstanding Jewish scholars were involved. The 13th Graduate School concentrated on the church and the people of Israel. A large pastors' and missionaries' course examined what Christians can learn, both positively and negatively, for their Christian mission from the Jewish presence among the nations.

Not all gatherings centred so strongly on church-world issues, but relatively few meetings were devoted to *inner church life*. A course for lay people with special financial and administrative responsibilities in local churches dealt with church administration and church renewal. A meeting with bishops, church presidents and other church leaders examined how ecclesiastical decisions are a test case for the ecumenical movement. Questions concerning the training of pastors and priests were gradually given greater importance in the Bossey programme. The series that began with the meetings involving church historians was continued with similar conferences for theological teachers, one each for those teaching ecumenics, New Testament, practical theology and systematic theology. The question of the ministry and the ministries of the church became the theme of a Graduate School and was often discussed in summer courses. The unity of the churches, interconfessional relations and the history of the ecumenical movement were of course prominent in many programmes of the Institute. Thus the changing relationship with the Roman Catholic Church was central in the 7th and 15th Graduate Schools.

To become a Christian presence in the world church members must be firmly *rooted in biblical faith*. Some of the summer courses therefore took up central affirmations of the creed. There were theological student courses on the resurrection, the ecumenical councils and the unity and diversity of Christian faith traditions. During the period of the pioneers corporate Bible study had a major role in all Bossey meetings. By the end of the 1950s and especially during the 1960s the need for biblical nurture and discernment had somehow become less self-evident. This was why special conferences and courses on Bible study were now organized at Bossey. In 1955 a consultation was jointly sponsored with the World Student Christian Federation at which participants looked at typical Orthodox, Protestant and Roman Catholic ways of studying and meditating on the Bible. Here too emphasis was laid on non-literary ways of Bible study, using the resources of oral communication, visual arts, drama and mime. In a conference on Bible reading notes and biblical theology participants critically examined various types of existing daily Bible reading notes and then were challenged to write short notes that would be exegetically responsible, easily readable and would help people to think and act biblically in their daily life and work in the secular world. In the late 1960s, when biblical authority was most seriously challenged, the staff and the board decided to take up this challenge and devote the 19th Graduate School to this theme.

The most essential part of Christian presence in the world does not consist in multiplying Christian actions and statements; it is *Christian spirituality open to the world* and constantly renewed in worship. The daily intercessory prayers at noon in the chapel focused on specific church-world issues and remembered former participants. Up to the mid-1960s adults and children of the resident staff used to gather for a weekly family worship. During several summer courses a short week-end retreat was part of the schedule: introduced through a meditation on Saturday morning, leading to a period of silence during the afternoon, evening and night, and culminating in a communion service on Sunday morning. With all the words spoken at Bossey, the frustrations of words translated, half understood or misunderstood, such a period of silence and meditation became for many a much-needed break and resource for a new involvement in ecumenical dialogues, and for a new commitment to their work at home.

Often the attempt was made corporately to prepare and celebrate, at the end of a course, *the closing worship as a liturgical summing up* of what had been learned and experienced, and to bring it before God. After a plenary session where the main tenor and sequence of the worship were discussed and finalized, the participants, working in groups, prepared the different parts of the service. One group would be asked to prepare the chapel in such a way that the arrangement would express symbolically the theme of the course. Another group prepared the prayers and specially composed sung responses; another, the main message which might be communicated in the form of a personal testimony, a dialogue or a mime; yet another, a special act of commitment and sending out. This was always a risky enterprise but it usually brought out many creative gifts and often became the most deeply remembered climax of the whole course.

Such corporately prepared ad hoc worship services enabled many to discover or rediscover the great treasures and symbolism of traditional liturgies. In this respect the annual *seminar on Orthodox worship and theology*, meeting for two weeks during the time of the Orthodox Passion and Easter celebrations, became particularly important. Such a seminar had been started by Leon Zander and other teachers of the Russian Orthodox St Sergius Institute in Paris and was initially attended mainly by German Protestant theological students. With the presence of Nissiotis at Bossey, in 1959 the seminar was taken over by the Ecumenical Institute. Participants spend a whole week, getting themselves introduced to the Orthodox liturgy, iconography, spirituality and liturgical theology. They then go to Paris to attend holy week Orthodox services. Gradually participants of these seminars were recruited from more and more confessions and continents. Through Orthodox worship many Protestants and Catholics learned to appreciate more deeply the cosmic dimensions of worship and gained the insight that worship is not only an important preparation for Christian presence in the world but is in itself an essential part of such presence.

How does one evaluate the results of this immensely diverse period of growth? What purpose did the staff see in *the constant gathering and sending out* of people in ever new Graduate Schools, conferences and courses? In the report presented to the WCC assembly in 1961, Wolf wrote in his usual self-critical way that one had to be very careful about the often spontaneously expressed enthusiasm with regard to the work of the Ecumenical Institute. Yes, such enthusiasm may grow out of "a new vision of the missionary church which is sometimes glimpsed in the meetings at Bossey, and, when seen, fills people with joy and quickens them with a readiness to return and work for the realization of that vision". But such enthusiasm may not endure.

> The real test of the Institute's work is whether those who shared in its courses and conferences return home to take up work for the renewal of their churches in a new way, with holy impatience and as collaborators in the ecumenical movement.

Seeing all these groups come and go, for many, especially for the resident staff, the *glass mosaic wall of the chapel* assumed a deep symbolic significance. When the sun shines through this wall the mosaic, without figures, becomes a feast of warm and cold tints of colours. In the panel near the altar the yellow flames of the Spirit, which may also be interpreted as praying hands or as ears of wheat, are brought together in a serene blue-white space: the church gathered for worship. When he conceived this mosaic the artist had in mind the old eucharistic prayer: "As this broken bread, once dispersed over the hills, was brought together and became one loaf, so may thy church be brought together from the ends of the earth into thy kingdom." In discussions with the directors a second theme soon surfaced and the wall received its second panel near the chapel door: the yellow flames or hands or ears of wheat are now scattered and half buried like good seed in the variously shaded field with its red road of strife and suffering: a Christian community which has been gathered for a while is being sent out into the world to witness, suffer and bear fruit.

5. Rethinking the Role of Bossey: 1970-1983

After 1968 Bossey perhaps would have lost touch with what was happening in the world, had it not itself gone through a series of crises which affected the life of the Institute for several years. In fact, after these crisis years Bossey was never the same again. It would be pointless to want to go back to the period of the pioneers and the succeeding years of development. The times had changed; so had the leadership, the questions people were asking and the tasks Bossey had to address.

A world learning to co-exist

During the years reviewed here, the oikoumene was marked by the *growing co-existence of the two power blocs*. In 1971 the People's Republic of China became a member of the United Nations. Two years later the president of the USA went to China, and also to the Soviet Union where the first Strategic Arms Limitation Treaty (SALT) was signed. In 1975 many states from the East and the West accepted the Helsinki declaration on security and cooperation in Europe. Only two weeks before that crucial meeting, a "summit" took place in space where a Soviet and a US space ship met, and astronauts from the two power blocs could undertake joint research: a symbol of the changing times.

Co-existence did not mean universal peace. *Local unrest* continued in many places, causing much suffering and an ever-increasing exodus of refugees. Nor was the gap bridged between the rich and the poor. The Middle East remained the most explosive region with a new conflict between Israel and Egypt and Syria, the chaos in Lebanon, the Soviet intervention in Afghanistan and the confrontation between Iraq and Iran. There was bitter disappointment in many parts of Africa when former heroes of liberation turned into dictators. Political upheaval and famines threatened the survival of millions. In Asia tensions in the Indian sub-continent led to political, religious and ethnic conflicts. The war in Vietnam, Cambodia and Laos continued even after the American troops were forced to leave. Latin and Central America suffered from galloping inflation, leading to military take-overs and dictatorships that promised to work for national security and economic development but ended up in the oppression of people and widespread violation of human rights. In Western Europe and North America daily life in many cities became insecure because of racial tension, violent demonstrations, and the rising levels of crime and terrorism.

Nevertheless, co-existence checked the threat of nuclear world war and gave room for hopeful developments. The dream of ushering in radical change ended in cynicism, but it also led to the long struggle of mobilizing world opinion and people's action against hunger, torture, racism and sexism. The year 1975 became the United Nation's Year of Women and 1979 the International Year of the Child. People's action was being organized to defend the rights of the marginalized and also to protect land, air and water from pollution. In Eastern Europe movements for a more democratic regime gathered momentum, as in Charter 77 declared in Prague in 1977 and the Solidarity trade union organized in Poland in 1980. The politically and economically mighty of this world had to yield once in a while to the power of the powerless. Thus in Southern Africa people's resistance could not be broken by torture or military force.

Two forces which deeply influenced the course of history in the 1970s were those of *oil and the American dollar*. With developing industries and growing road and air traffic, there was increasing demand for energy, especially for oil. The oil-producing nations began, from 1971 onwards, to use oil as a means of exercising political pressure. Western companies in the Middle East were nationalized, prices doubled and oil embargoes declared. This oil crisis revealed the vulnerability of the whole economic industrial set-up. In the early 1970s the American dollar was devalued. The floating exchange rates led to a new world financial crisis, strongly affecting international organizations. There was a growing recognition that the continuing population growth and industrial production led to the deterioration of the natural environment and that the risk of ecological catastrophes was real. The nuclear accident on Three Mile Island in the USA shook the confidence of people that the production of nuclear energy was safe.

Above: Nikos Nissiotis, centre, with students

Left: Relaxing with a game of volley ball

A corner of the dining hall

Karl Hertz
(photo L'Osservatore Romano/
Arturo Mari)

Right: The totem pole

Adriaan Geense

John Mbiti

Jacques Nicole with students in the lecture hall

The library

The chapel

The growing computerization of machines led to upsetting uncertainties about the role of *work and leisure*. For increasing production and consumption human labour was seen as being too slow and too expensive. Production had to be "rationalized". This meant that in many industrial centres unemployment grew, affecting first the millions of migrant workers who had come from rural backgrounds and poor countries to industrial areas. Gradually more qualified workers and employees too became victims of unemployment. Potentially the machines could liberate women, men and children from repetitive and dehumanizing labour, allowing time for human fellowship, creative activities and learning. A minority indeed used the new situation in such positive ways. But the available technologies and the media had done little to bridge the gap between the rich and the poor, and for the majority of people loss of work led only to a loss of identity and to unnecessary consumption. The quest for meaning in life had become ever more urgent.

Changes and reviews

The wave of protests in the late 1960s had its impact on Bossey only in the early 1970s. For radical West Europeans *the year 1968* had quite other connotations than for students coming from Eastern Europe. Many of the Asian and African participants came to Bossey out of different and deeper revolutions than the wordy ones on Western campuses. For the boards and the teaching staff of a world institute, located in Europe and related to a European university, the situation now was highly complex. How seriously should they take the demands of mainly Western protesters? Were Western radicals the prophets of the new age, or were they only imposing a new type of Western imperialism on an international group? Which of the world's agendas was Bossey to follow?

There was clearly a *generation gap*. Those who mainly shaped the Institute's programme, the members of the two boards, the Bossey director and associate director, were one or two generations older than most participants of the Graduate School and the student courses. As in many educational institutions, in politics and in the whole of society, there was tension, and often a lack of dialogue, between the older and the younger generations. In fact conferences with restless young people had been held at Bossey in the late 1960s to discuss exactly this generation gap; yet more was needed than conferences.

The 1970-71 Graduate School left the last five weeks free for full student participation in the shaping of the programme. The result was that 28 different subjects were proposed of which finally eight were selected to be dealt with in groups. The selection process involved endless days of debate, not for deciding *what* to study but for discussing *how* to decide. Finally, little time was left for doing any serious study. Because of the unpopular subject — the Bible — that whole semester was a difficult enterprise. Conservative participants felt that historical critical methods of study undermined Christian faith and biblical authority. Radicals considered these same methods as a bourgeois way of doing theology. The two boards made long evaluations. Should the subjects chosen always conform to current fashion? Where was the dividing line between the necessary safeguarding of tradition and study disciplines on the one hand, and the equally necessary change providing for fuller student participation in decision-making on the other? During the Graduate Schools of the next three years questioning and criticism grew even more severe — students against one another, against the Bossey establishment and against the weak input from the World Council headquarters. Regular community worship life and common Bible studies became almost impossible. Protest at times took the form of staying away or the non-participation of silence, a confrontation more difficult to deal with than open revolt.

Everything seemed to be changing. In the Bossey programme too the theme of change predominated in the early 1970s. The 20th Graduate School dealt with participation in change and several summer courses treated subjects related to this situation of change. Together with the Council's Humanum Studies, Bossey organized in the early 1970s interdisciplinary consultations on the human capacity for change and on ways human institutions relate to change.

In his last two reports to the Bossey board Nikos Nissiotis pointed to two characteristics of the new mood which the Institute had to face in this transitional period. First, ecumenism was changing. Intercultural encounters were now given priority over interconfessional ones and there was a shift not only from dogmatics to ethics but also from social ethics to political ethics. Second, the educational process was changing. The content-knowledge orientation was being replaced by a doing-knowledge orientation. All teaching methods were suspect as entailing conscious or unconscious oppression and the aim of education was primarily seen as conscientization. How could Bossey positively respond to this new mood without losing valuable insights and traditions inherited from the past?

No wonder that within five years the Institute went through no fewer than *three review processes*. In 1971 the board, since 1969 chaired by Hans-Heinrich Harms, evaluated Bossey's past and present work. It prepared an essentially affirmative statement for the group which had been appointed to look at priorities and a new structure for the whole World Council. In spite of that evaluation, the very next year a Committee of Five was asked to make a much more thorough review of Bossey's work. It was chaired by Theressa Hoover from the USA and its members were the Romanian Orthodox bishop Anthonie, the Dutch philosopher C.A. van Peursen, the Japanese theologian Kosuke Koyama and the Zambian layman Jason Mfula. The committee did an excellent job of listening and assessing, making helpful suggestions for the future. The report did not deal with finance (which was not part of the mandate), and many of its suggestions were shelved — at a time when the very existence of the Institute had become uncertain. Just before the Nairobi assembly of the World Council in 1975 an emergency group was asked to go into the possibilities for Bossey to survive, in one way or another, and to advise the WCC governing bodies about decisions to be taken. This, as we shall see, was not the end of the reviewing process.

It is astonishing that in the midst of all the uncertainties, staff changes and extra work which reviewing processes involve, the Bossey programme continued. The Graduate School and the Orthodox seminar too continued to be held year after year, large summer courses were organized, specialized interdisciplinary conferences prepared and conducted, often leading to substantial reports.

New Bossey teams

The period of transition meant many staff changes. Within just thirteen years three persons with totally different backgrounds and gifts were entrusted with the main leadership of the Institute. For the everyday life at Bossey equally upsetting was the departure of two persons who had helped with the running of the house over a long period and whose presence meant so much during the critical change-overs from one director to another — Simone Mathil and Herman de Graaf. With their departure Bossey lost much of its "memory" and long-term perspectives.

Not less devoted were the *support and house staff* who took over from these veterans of Bossey. The librarian, Margret Koch, helped at times also as seminar leader. Among the interpreters Margaret Pater served for a second long period and was of great help to many. Since the 1970s Roswitha Ginglas and Evelyne Tatu have been the interpreters, making communication possible at meeting after meeting. The main responsibilities of the office were carried for a time by Adrienne Reber and later by Sheila Ray and her colleagues. John McVie served for many years as accountant. The key position for hospitality was held by a succession of people until Marianne Dessoulavy became the *gouvernante* (housekeeper). The post of associate director for administration was created in 1978 and Ed Ph. van der Burgh served in that position for six years. With his previous experience in a national youth centre he took many initiatives to develop Bossey into an attractive guest house and conference centre.

In 1971 *the teaching team* consisted of Nikos Nissiotis, Hans-Ruedi Weber and Michael Keeling. Increasing responsibilities outside Bossey made it difficult for Nissiotis to attend to all the day-to-day concerns, though he gave leadership to three more Graduate Schools and several summer courses and interdisciplinary conferences. Weber was already in the process of taking up a new assignment at the World Council headquarters, and about this time Keeling returned to Great Britain.

The person who in an unassuming way carried the Institute through the troubled period was *Alain Blancy*, from 1971 to 1981 associate director. From a Jewish-Christian family, he grew up in Berlin, whence he emigrated to France and became a pastor of the French Reformed Church. He served in various parishes, and held leadership positions in educational institutions. Marginalized as a Jew in Germany and as a German in France, and with his concentration camp background, he could empathize with Bossey participants coming from areas of cultural and political upheaval. With his great intellectual curiosity and good knowledge of theology he devoted himself to all aspects of life and teaching at the Institute. Because of him some of the best thinkers of the French-speaking world could be brought into Bossey's interdisciplinary work. Many of the Institute's support staff and helpers in the house remember Blancy in the first place as the pastor. After leaving Bossey, he became the pastor of a local congregation, but continued to be extensively involved in ecumenical work in the French-speaking world.

After Anwar Barkat's early return to Pakistan Bossey worked again with only three members on its teaching staff. Then *outside sponsorships* from America and Germany made it possible to appoint two short-term assistant directors. This pattern of financing members of teaching staff from sources outside the World Council budget became regular. It helps the Institute to survive but is not without its dangers, and it can unduly influence policies. Both new appointees were specialists for interdisciplinary work. One, Gert von Wahlert from Germany, was a student of biology; he stayed only for a year and then took up research work in maritime biology.

A young Japanese professor of law, *Rihito Kimura*, joined Bossey in 1972 and worked there for four years. He had been involved in student work and teaching in Thailand, and had taught comparative law at Saigon university when life in Vietnam was still in turmoil. He brought to Bossey once again the realities of Asia and Asian ways of thinking and doing things. Kimura was involved mostly in conferences on justice and human rights. After Bossey he continued his teaching ministry in Asia and later in North America.

By the early 1970s it became clear that intercultural theology would be a major emphasis in the Institute's future work. Looking for a new director the board decided that it should be a theologian from Africa or Asia who was deeply immersed in a non-Western society, doing creative theology within the thought patterns of that culture. The new director should be fully qualified both for continuing the dialogue with representatives of traditional theologies inherited from the Eastern and Western church and also encourage development of contextual theologies in other cultures. To find such a person took longer than anticipated.

The search was over in 1974, when *John S. Mbiti* joined Bossey. He taught at the Institute for six years. Growing up in an African village society in a pious Christian family, Mbiti had become interested in rethinking the Christian faith in the light of African philosophy and African oral cultural traditions. During his studies in Uganda, the USA and Great Britain, where he also served as an Anglican priest, he concentrated on biblical theology and on the analysis of African concepts of life. Mbiti was married to a Swiss social worker, and they and their children experienced daily an intercultural reality. Before coming to Bossey Mbiti had taught at the department of religious studies and philosophy in Makerere university at Kampala. There he had become head of the department, published a number of scholarly articles and books on African religion and the relationship between the gospel and African culture.

At Bossey Mbiti's major contributions were in the field of inter-cultural theology. In the late 1970s he held the largest and geographi-cally most representative specialized conferences in the Institute's history. Those who came to know and love this humble — in the best sense of that word — and pious man came to see in him not only the scholar but also the poet and story-teller. For one thing, however, Mbiti was ill prepared; the tough administrative and political task of directing the Institute during those turbulent years of change. Some-body else had to be appointed to do this task so that Mbiti could devote himself to teaching. After leaving Bossey, Mbiti became a pastor of the Reformed Church in German-speaking Switzerland and professor at Bern university.

Bossey had to get a senior person to direct its work, somebody like the president of a complex educational institution. *Karl H. Hertz* from the USA, a pastor and theological teacher of the Lutheran Church of America, was invited to join the Institute. During the world war he had served as a medical technician on the European fronts and been involved in giving medical care to persons released from concentra-tion camps. He then embarked on a long academic career, writing about and teaching sociology and social ethics at various American universities and seminaries. For the 26th Graduate School Hertz was a visiting lecturer, and at that time he and his wife had fallen in love with Bossey. Taking over as chief director in 1978, Hertz served at Bossey until his retirement in 1983.

The main contribution of Hertz was the carrying through of changes in the administration of the Institute as decided upon by the board and the World Council governing bodies. This required both firmness and tact, as well as experience in negotiating with commit-tees, in establishing new working relations with other educational institutions and in helping with financial campaigns. For much of this Hertz was the right man. Under his firm direction the Bossey pro-gramme could continue despite reduced budgets. He initiated work for planned publications on the history of Bossey. Hertz was the one who invited sisters of the Protestant religious community of Grandchamp to come during Graduate Schools and maintain a liturgical and pastoral presence among the students.

A new member of the teaching team under Hertz was the German Reformed theologian, *Hans Goedeking*. He worked at Bossey for eight years, beginning in 1976. His studies had centred on relating theology to the scientific/technological world and he had experience in pastoral work with students and parishes in industrial regions of Western Germany. Unfortunately his work started at the Institute just when frontier conferences in this special field had been abandoned. He suffered a stroke, and for a long time he could only carry a limited load of work. Goedeking had a deep impact on participants of Bossey courses because of the courage and spiritual strength with which he and his family faced his illness. During conferences on the churches' healing ministry his very presence gave a special dimension. After his time in Bossey Goedeking went back to pastoral work in Germany.

Since the beginning of the Institute there had been an *Orthodox presence* on the board and among visiting lecturers. After Nissiotis's return to Greece a young Greek Orthodox New Testament scholar, Johannes Panagopoulos, worked in Bossey for a short period as tutor, giving leadership to Orthodox seminars and biblical consultations. Then for over four years Bossey had no Orthodox theologian on its resident staff. The Orthodox task force at the Geneva headquarters, especially its moderator Georges Tsetsis, saw to it that Orthodox perspectives were not lacking in the Institute's teaching, and Blancy took over responsibility for the Orthodox seminar.

In 1980 *Dan-Ilie Ciobotea* from Romania joined the Bossey staff. He had just completed studies in Orthodox, Protestant and Roman Catholic theological faculties and his main research was on the relationship between theology and spirituality. Nissiotis and Panagopoulos were lay theologians and thinkers. During his time at Bossey Ciobotea became a monk and was ordained as a priest. He not only taught but lived Orthodox spirituality. In 1988 he was called back to Romania for higher ecclesiastical duties, and became Metropolitan Daniel.

Through several participants, speakers and resource persons a *Roman Catholic presence* had been established at Bossey from the early years. For a long time John Lucal, a Catholic priest working in international organizations in Geneva, lived at Bossey and contributed much to its intellectual and worship life. But there was still no Roman Catholic member of the resident teaching team. From the late 1960s a representative of the Catholic theological faculty of Fribourg university had served as a member of the board and good working relations with Fribourg had developed. Only a decade later could more official relationships with the Vatican be established. A week in Rome became part of the Graduate School programme, and the Secretariat for Promoting Christian Unity now sponsored a Roman Catholic theologian to serve as a tutor in the Graduate School. The first to serve thus was Maria Teresa Porcile Santiso, a biblical theologian from Uruguay.

Further church-world issues

During the first half of the 1970s Bossey still had a crowded programme. In between the Graduate Schools the large annual summer courses for pastors/priests and missionaries and for theological students continued, now with less frequent courses for lay people. The annual Orthodox seminar was held with varying numbers of participants who, from 1974 onwards, no longer went to Paris to participate in Orthodox Easter celebrations, and instead attended the liturgies in the Geneva region. The former sessions with theological professors for discovering the ecumenical dimension of a particular theological discipline were continued through meetings with younger tutors and lecturers of theological faculties, introducing them to the ecumenical movement. In addition to all these, interdisciplinary conferences pursued the topics of the 1960s, adding new explorations to them (see appendix C).

The *major thrust of educational courses* remained the search for a genuine Christian life and witness in a changing world that was becoming increasingly secularized. How can believers live and plan within the perspective of the promised kingdom in a world which plans along the lines of a programmed future? How can life remain truly human in the modern cities where decisions have to be made in a milieu of violence? The themes of the 20th, 21st, 22nd and 24th Graduate Schools reflected such questioning. There was also a great hunger for new kinds of communities and spiritualities; in large summer courses Blancy brought together Christians from the margins of official parishes and church structures who were looking for new forms of Christian fellowship in the world.

Within this changing world the question about the *continuity of faith* was at stake. For many people "God-language" had become incomprehensible and biblical affirmations had lost much of their authority. This led to a series of meetings with philosophers, systematic and biblical theologians, organized by Nissiotis in collaboration with David Jenkins who was in charge of the Council's Humanum Studies. How do dogmatic and contextual theologies relate to one another? How does dogma deal with change and what is the relationship between institutions and change? Summer courses were held on how to study the Bible in this questioning world and how to understand and transmit what the churches teach about "salvation" and "transcendence". Under the leadership of Panagopoulos biblical theologians and representatives of action groups examined what prophetic action means today in the light of the prophetic vocation in the New Testament and how the justice of God relates to human struggles for justice.

In the light of what was happening in the world new thinking was needed to respond to questions concerning *industry and the impact of science and technology.* Keeling gathered economists, people involved in industry and social ethicists in order to look critically at issues related to industrial production. It led to a new series of explorations led mainly by Blancy. A consultation with ecologists, economists and theologians examined the price of progress. According to the report of the meeting, an attempt was made to look at three inter-related concerns: first "the 'ecological' awareness and demands stimulated by the present environmental crisis"; second, "the no less acute struggle for social justice through development"; third, "the 'ecumenical' level in order to emphasize the fact that there can be no escape for the churches from such problems". The hope was that from this approach new insights and impulses might emerge "to revise the current concepts and practices which, based on the ambiguous term 'progress', have led to the present dilemma, the 'price' of which was to be assessed".

In the following two meetings in this series questions of *power and human identity* were addressed. Sociologists and philosophers joined the economists and ecologists to examine such issues as power and property in the use of world resources and human identity in nature, science and society. The concluding conference worked in groups on three different levels of human interaction: language, economics and culture. The first looked at the ways of perceiving reality — that of "explaining" in scientific language and that of "understanding" in faith language. A second group explored the relationship between scarcity and conflict, taking as an example the context of the world food crisis. The third group examined the impact of Western technology on different cultures.

Another series of interdisciplinary meetings continued the reflection on *law, international relations and human rights*, with input from specialists in social ethics. The subject of penal policies was discussed by criminologists, psychologists and prison administrators called together by Keeling. In connection with all the other consultations on change lawyers and sociologists took up the theme of law and social change. This led to further gatherings, directed mainly by Kimura and Blancy on the role of law in the service of human needs, followed by two conferences on fundamental human rights. The series ended with a meeting on self-reliance and solidarity in the quest for international justice.

In all these interdisciplinary conferences there was some *overlap with ongoing WCC studies*. With different priorities and study methods the WCC department on Church and Society, the Commission on the Churches' Participation in Development and the joint WCC/Vatican committee on Society, Development and Peace were involved in the fields of economics, science and technology. The Churches' Commission on International Affairs had been dealing for years with questions of law and international justice. These programmes participated in the Bossey meetings and partly helped to finance them. Nevertheless, the question could be asked whether the Bossey conferences on such subjects were not an irresponsible duplication of work.

Many of those who sat in World Council study commissions and participated also in the Institute's interdisciplinary encounters commented on the unique character of the Bossey meetings. The setting of the Institute, its regular worship life, the role of the blue angels, the availability of a library and the life together not in a hotel or a conference centre but in a place at the heart of the ecumenical movement created a special atmosphere. Here at Bossey the ways of working were less formal than those of the more official Council meetings which usually had to work under pressure to produce agreed statements. The encounters at the Institute could at times bring together the concerns of different WCC departmental studies and provide feed-back to them. For Bossey itself the interdisciplinary conferences were essential to remain sensitive to the world's agenda. They also greatly enriched the teaching in Graduate Schools and summer courses. Nevertheless, this frontier work was the first part of Bossey's work to be questioned and dropped when the budget had to be cut. Only very few interdisciplinary conferences were organized in the "Bossey style" after 1976. In the new formulation of the aim and functions of the Institute accepted in 1977 such frontier work is not even mentioned.

To be or not to be

Instead of the usual December circular letter of "Bossey News", Mbiti sent in October 1975 a letter *sounding the alarm* to former participants and friends of the Institute. The officers of the World Council had just proposed to its governing bodies that the Ecumenical Institute be closed down by 30 June 1976 unless it could cover its own budget. Subsidies from the general WCC budget would no longer be available. This came as a shock to many. People knew that, mainly owing to the dollar crisis, the WCC was in a desperate financial situation. From 1971 onwards a few members of the governing bodies had questioned the very existence of Bossey, and it was clear that extra-budgetary funds and sponsored staff positions would have to be found for the work of the Institute to continue. But now the proposal was to drop Bossey from the WCC budget! Almost as if the Institute were not part of the Council!

Radical cuts were imperative. But where? It became a *question of priorities*. Behind the financial crisis was a deep identity crisis, for both Bossey and the Council, in addition to personality conflicts among staff and committees. For almost thirty years Bossey had pioneered and had often been seen as innovative and radical. Now, especially after the Geneva world conference on Church and Society in 1966, the Council's governing bodies seemed to have become more radical in their approach. Had Bossey not become a bourgeois establishment, catering to an elite, living in an academic ivory tower, away from the urgent battles of faith in the present world? If the Institute were located somewhere in Latin America or Africa where people's struggles were a part of hope, or in an Asian region where Christians daily meet people of other living faiths and ideologies, then such an institution might serve the ecumenical cause better than in the château, isolated from the world, in a peaceful Swiss rural environment. Was Bossey "a holy cow" which could not be touched? Some 800,000 Swiss francs would immediately be saved if Bossey were dropped from the general budget. If let out on rent or sold it would become an additional source of income for the Council. To face such basic questions was tough but also a healthy test for Bossey. The Council's executive committee and General Secretariat did not evade such questioning, nor did they want to make premature decisions. The Council's assembly had to decide on priorities.

Before the assembly met in Nairobi an emergency group, chaired by W.A. Visser 't Hooft, presented in November 1975 a *survival plan for Bossey*, offering concrete options. A month later, at the assembly itself, an action of support was launched among the participants with a public announcement: "In order to manifest their gratitude and their attachment to the Ecumenical Institute by a concrete sign a number of participants in this assembly have decided to make a personal contribution to start a fund which will provide additional income... Pledges should be handed in at the reception desk." This action brought in some 50,000 Swiss francs. Assembly discussions also indicated that church representatives wanted the work of Bossey to be continued and to be kept within the Council.

The new executive committee of the Council decided to allow a time for rethinking and restructuring. Never in the Institute's history were more letters written, more proposals made and more committees convened to discuss the future of the Institute than in that period after Nairobi. Among those who organized this campaign and rethinking were members of the new board, its moderator, Paul Crow from the American Disciples of Christ, and François Bovon from the Geneva theological faculty playing a prominent role. Among the Council's headquarters staff both Lukas Vischer from Faith and Order and Konrad Raiser from the General Secretariat gave much time and energy for what was sometimes called "the battle for Bossey". Raiser was for a few months acting director of the Institute, between the directorships of Mbiti and Hertz. Financial support came mainly from Germany, Switzerland, France, Holland and the USA. The budget of Bossey was cut down. This obviously meant also a reduction of programme and staff. Specially designated contributions from churches and individuals, sponsored salaries and a continuing though reduced subsidy from the WCC general budget made it possible for the Institute to survive during the crisis years. With a view to long term needs, a Bossey Endowment Fund was launched. The target was ten million Swiss francs. That was never realized, but as early as 1977 one million had been received.

New by-laws concerning the *status, aim and functions of the Institute* were accepted by the Council's governing bodies in 1977. Discussions on the status rejected the proposal that Bossey become a separate legal entity or an independent foundation. The Institute remained "a specialized unit of the WCC". Its aim was

> to contribute to the formation of future generations of ecumenical leadership, among both clergy and laity; to provide for ecumenical theological encounter in an intercultural and interconfessional setting; and to build community in which ecumenical experience and different kinds of spirituality are being shared and ecumenical understanding nurtured.

The five functions are first the Graduate School, followed by the organization of courses and consultations, cooperation with ecumenical partner institutions and centres of ecumenical education and research, extension work, and the provision of a centre for meetings.

The by-laws also stipulated a restructuring of the organization. The programme section for activities sponsored and co-sponsored by Bossey was separated from the guest section related to the management of the Institute as a meeting place. The director and members of the teaching staff (now called lecturers) were to be responsible for programme; an administrative associate director would be responsible for the guest house section. A single board would carry responsibility for all affairs of the Institute.

In 1978 a *new agreement between the WCC and Geneva university* was signed, replacing the 1951 one between the Council and the autonomous theological faculty in Geneva university. Until then the relationship had concerned only the Graduate School and the faculty. The new agreement provided for a link between the total work of the Institute and the university. Actual collaboration happened on the level of the faculty rather than that of the students. Directors of Bossey continued to give some lectures at the theological faculty and professors of Geneva occasionally taught at Bossey. This was especially the case for Orthodox and Roman Catholic ecumenists who were invited by Geneva university for guest lectureships. One of them, Yves Congar, even stayed at Bossey while lecturing in Geneva.

For planning, organizing and financing the Bossey programme *various forms of partnerships* were sought. The Institute and the Council's sub-units had always maintained an informal cooperation. Now these working relationships were intensified and more institutionalized. Partnerships with other academic institutions, ecumenical organizations and centres were explored. Some common work thus developed with the Lutheran World Federation, the Orthodox Centre in Chambésy, the Roman Catholic theological faculty at Fribourg university and with the Vatican Secretariat for Promoting Christian Unity. From the late 1970s onwards it becomes difficult to distinguish clearly a specific Bossey initiative and contribution in the Institute's programme from what came from such partners.

A strong emphasis was laid on the development of *extension work* which had already begun with the Bossey courses in Berlin and a few meetings in Finland and Lebanon. What "extension" actually meant remained vague. The report of the Committee of Five spoke about "mobility". It suggested that members of the Bossey teaching staff might occasionally accept work assignments in regional ecumenical centres or that participants of the Graduate School might be gathered in their own regions before or after the Bossey semester for briefing and debriefing sessions. In the late 1970s Blancy and Mbiti made exploratory visits to Africa and Asia with a view to developing "Bossey" courses in partnership with ecumenical centres in these regions. Similar plans were made for North and Latin America. All these projects too could not make much headway because of the tight financial situation.

In the various review processes before and after the Nairobi assembly great emphasis was laid on *ecumenical education*, later called *ecumenical learning*. From its origin Bossey had of course fostered such learning through worship, community life and teaching. Ecumenical learning for the most part happened spontaneously and without conscious planning. In the late 1960s the educational sub-units of the Council developed much thinking on the dynamics of ecumenical learning, its theory and practice, inspired principally by Ernst Lange. One of the criticisms voiced by the Council headquarters staff was that Bossey did not sufficiently plan the ecumenical learning process in planning the programmes for the Graduate School and the summer courses. Consequently, in 1982 the sub-unit on Education and the Ecumenical Institute organized together a workshop on education for effective ecumenism.

The Graduate School as the backbone

None of the several review groups which discussed and planned the future of Bossey suggested that the Graduate School should be discontinued. On the contrary, the school is called *the primary task of the Institute* and in the various versions of the functions of Bossey it comes first. The Committee of Five even suggested that the school period be lengthened to six months or a full academic year with some time devoted to language studies, a long semester at Bossey, followed by field-work. This was never implemented, but the trend at that time was to lengthen rather than shorten the academic course.

The Graduate School had become an institution. To gather annually some fifty participants from all continents and major Christian confessions requires a long process of recruitment and selection. In addition much time-consuming work must be done to secure the necessary finance and scholarships, plan the programme and then get the key lecturers and (preferably seconded) tutors. Almost every year some experimentation was attempted to secure a better structure for the schedule and to try out more participatory ways of teaching and learning. On the whole, however, the Graduate School now had a basic pattern and purpose. In 1976 the board defined it as follows:

> The specific focus of the Graduate School in the context of the total programme of the Ecumenical Institute is to foster theological education in ecumenical perspective. This includes developing ways of "doing theology" which integrate reflection and action, study and spiritual life, and take the contextual character of all theology seriously into account.

Despite its two-decade history and tradition *every Graduate School remained an event*, in the first place for the participants but also for the resident staff. All that was said in the last chapter about this event- and experience-character of such a semester could be said also for the period under consideration: the initial feeling of being a stranger; the slow growth of community through periods of crisis, hurt and reconciliation; the discovery of one's own confessional and cultural background with its limitations and its richness; the meeting with the liturgy and spirituality of the Orthodox churches; and above all the excitement of a transcultural encounter.

The newness of each Graduate School comes first of all from the ever new composition of the group of participants. A list of participants in the 1st to the 30th semester shows the gradual growth of student strength from 20 to over 60. It also shows the slow but steady increase in the number of students from Asia and Africa. Europeans and North Americans were often a minority, as Latin Americans had always been. From the late 1970s Bossey had participants from the Pacific islands who enriched its life with their special cultures and spiritualities which emphasize celebration and community building. Confessionally the Protestant tradition still had the majority, but both with regard to teachers and participants the Orthodox and Roman Catholic presence now became steadily stronger. Most participants were theologically trained and the number of graduates of other disciplines remained small. The percentage of women increased to about a quarter, sometimes a third, of the student body.

For the teaching staff newness came from the ever-changing *main themes* (see appendix A). A slight shift of emphasis can be noticed from the mid-1970s onwards, studies dealing essentially with church-world issues becoming less prominent than studies on Christ, on the Spirit and on the life, unity and ministries of the churches. The report of the Committee of Five had proposed the choice of the same theme for two successive semesters, after a consultation on it with the speakers of the two Graduate Schools. This was not implemented and only from the mid-1980s would two semesters occasionally deal with the same theme.

An important innovation since 1978 was the *week in Rome* at the end of the semester. This complemented the continuing visits to Swiss parishes and the visit to the Taizé community. The stay in Rome was made financially and organizationally possible through the growing cooperation with the Vatican Secretariat for Promoting Christian Unity. The week's programme provided for sessions with various Vatican secretariats, and with Roman Catholic lay movements and communities. Since 1980 the week normally included a special audience with the pope. There have also been visits to ancient Christian sites such as the Roman catacombs and a meeting with Protestant teachers and students of the Waldensian theological faculty.

Since the early 1980s, the presence at Bossey of two *sisters of the community of Grandchamp* near Neuchâtel has made a great contribution to the worship and spiritual life of the Graduate School. This

Protestant sisterhood has links with the Taizé brotherhood in France, but it has developed its own way of serving the ecumenical cause through worship and retreats and a Christian presence in the world. The sisters have a great openness to Orthodox and Roman Catholic spirituality while they maintain their Protestant identity. For the Graduate School, a temporary learning and worshipping fellowship, the presence of two resident sisters who exemplify in their day-to-day life an ecumenically open and informed spirituality has been of great importance; they help the diverse group of participants to grow into a rhythm of worship and work. They also do what for the busy teaching team always remains difficult, and are always present and available with friendship and pastoral sensitivity for both participants and the house staff, especially for those who feel marginalized or pass through spiritual struggles.

These were encouraging developments, but in certain areas there was stagnation. The *field-work programme* never really took off. From the early 1970s the debriefing week at Bossey was dropped because of financial constraints. Field-work requires much skill and a good deal of time for supervision which the teaching team did not have. Hertz therefore proposed in his last report to the board that such an extension of the semester be dropped unless it could be better organized.

In the area of *ecumenical research* in connection with the Graduate School there was little progress. Only few candidates submitted diploma papers. The ecumenical doctoral programme stagnated almost totally. Several new candidates started research work in this field with a view to submitting a doctoral dissertation to Bossey and Geneva university, but after 1971 only two managed to complete their studies.

Not all Graduate Schools were as difficult as those of the early 1970s. Nevertheless, there was *continuing criticism*. Despite better advance information about what to expect students still came with very different expectations. In spite of more careful selection of candidates, in almost every semester there were students who did not fully meet the admission requirements. Despite fewer lectures and more input from participants, especially in seminars, the right balance between teaching and learning remained difficult to achieve. Outside lecturers still did not stay long enough with the group. The quality of information given by headquarters staff on ongoing work at the World

Council continued to be a point of criticism. Most difficult to achieve was a balance among three different learning processes: the ecumenical experience of everyday life, mediated through the laughter and pain and the times of worship and fellowship in community life; the corporate study of a broad, ecumenically important theme; the introduction to ecumenical history and present-day ecumenical programmes of study and action. The Graduate School thus remained at once an impossible goal and yet a stimulating reality — and for many an experience of conversion.

"We have participated in an experience that will have profound effect on us throughout our lives." With this sentence begins the corporate booklet *Unity: Sharing Diversity* through which members of the 26th semester shared the "Bossey event" with others. The 62 students from 30 countries and all continents had lived together, studying the theme "Church, state and power". Some had come because that theme was of crucial importance for them in their daily life and ministry at home. Others had come because they wanted to experience a fully interconfessional and intercultural encounter. One cannot live in such a milieu without being changed. The booklet contains little on the studies around the theme. What impressed the participants more deeply were the experiences they had together, the joys and fears they shared with one another.

> Problems in far-off countries became personal as we lived, ate and prayed with those who are directly affected by those events. From a devastating cyclone in India to the banning of Christian organizations in South Africa, the immediate impact was that these events are happening to human beings and that they call for a response from each of us, because in some way, these problems have also become our own.

Many factors lead to growth. Through corporate study of the theme, common worship according to different traditions, and above all through personal meetings and conversations, almost every member of the group finds that the theological, confessional and cultural presuppositions which one had taken for granted are suddenly called in question. In the journey of ecumenical learning one cannot continue from where one stands; one must go back to the essentials, and then one is often led along a path which one does not want to take. "While none of us are ever completely free of our past, we were relatively free of the roles we were expected to play at home." Change then came through much internal conflict as each of us had to look critically at our own life, faith and attitudes in terms of the experience here. But the result of this searching is growth and in some way we each became a new person, not separate from the old but with new dimensions to that person.

Many participants come by *learning in surprising ways*. A mature African who at home is a respected chief may experience a moment of truth when he is expected to do "women's work" like washing up dishes after a meal. A brilliant young European student may suddenly be interrupted in his learned discourse on Christology by an Asian who has recently been imprisoned for fighting for justice in his country: "Yes, but what do you *believe*?" The participants of the 26th semester had a time of learning when at the birthday party of an American student the tape recorder broke down. With no dance music the evening, it appeared, was ruined. Then an African began tapping a rhythm on a table. Others joined in with improvised musical instruments.

As a guitar and a violin were added the mood very quickly changed and the enthusiasm spread as more people became involved. When the recorder was finally repaired it was not turned on and the so-called "ruined party" continued until 3 o'clock in the morning. This gave us a new understanding of what ecumenical sharing means.

Intercultural theology

After its hard struggle for survival the Institute could now run only a reduced summer programme. Outside groups and other guest house activities filled much of the time in between the Graduate Schools. The practice of scheduling two or more courses (co-)sponsored by Bossey immediately one after another started in 1977, and was an excellent innovation. To a limited extent it implemented a proposal made much earlier — to have at Bossey a one- or two-month summer school of ecumenics. Participants could register either for just one course or for the whole series.

As with the Graduate School themes, the subjects of these *summer courses and conferences* also reveal a slight shift from a world-centred to a more church-centred emphasis. The renewal and emerging shapes of church life and questions related to the churches' worship, prayer and unity now came to the fore. The healing ministry was emphasized, especially in courses directed by Hertz and Goedeking.

Courses prepared by Blancy concentrated on ecumenical ethics and spirituality. The world's agenda was not forgotten. Always in collaboration with World Council sub-units and other partners there were meetings on children and family life, church-state relationships, peaceful resolution of conflicts, and ecumenical concerns in relation to nuclear energy.

Undoubtedly the Institute's most creative work during the second half of the 1970s was done in the field of *gospel, faiths and cultures*. Every culture has at its heart a creed, which is expressed and transmitted by cults and rites. To do Christian theology in the context of different cultures inevitably means therefore to come into dialogue with people of other living faiths. The 21st Graduate School had already concentrated on such interfaith dialogue with speakers and resource persons from Jewish, Muslim, Hindu, secular humanist and Marxist backgrounds. The Hindu speaker, B. Mukerji, who stayed with the group for the whole semester, became the "guru" for many. The theme of that semester was too broad and too heavy for most participants. Moreover, a deep dialogue requires more than speakers from different faith communities; it can happen only when people belonging to various faith communities live together for a period, and grow in the understanding of one another's creed, cult and culture.

This happened at Bossey meetings that promoted *encounters of Christians and Jews*. From 1949 the relationship between these two faith communities had figured on the programme of the Institute and Jewish scholars were periodically invited to lecture and lead Bible studies. In 1978 a further step was taken. With the help of partners Bossey gathered some thirty Christians, worshipping in the chapel, and about thirty Jews, worshipping in the "salon blanc" where the Torah had been placed. Meals came from a kosher restaurant. The lectures dealt with the role of human beings in creation, society and history, always seen from a Jewish and a Christian perspective, and there was much space for group and personal conversations. In the report Mbiti said that despite the sad events happening at that very time in Israel and Lebanon the initial "fear and suspicion melted away and gave way to an atmosphere of real friendship and openness". The seminar ended with a corporate "period of silent prayer and praise, at which one felt a deep sense of God's presence and working among us".

Almost inevitably the Christian-Jewish dialogue leads also to a *dialogue between Christians and Muslims*. Together with a colleague from the Council's sub-unit on dialogue Goedeking organized a youth seminar on what faith means in a changing world. About one third of the participants were Muslims. Such interfaith dialogue must in the first place happen at the local level where people daily live and work together. A place like Bossey, where people are relatively free from the roles they are expected to play at home, can prepare them for such encounters — which pose today the most fundamental questions to Christian believers and theologians.

For entering into dialogue with people of other faiths Christians must first of all learn from *Christian interconfessional and intercultural dialogue*. Much has been done since the early 20th century in the area of mutual teaching and learning among Christians of different confessions. This often included also, however unconsciously, a dialogue of cultures, because behind the Eastern Orthodox and the Western Catholic/Protestant traditions lie deep cultural differences. A new sensitivity to the cultural factor and the whole gospel-culture debate are of extreme importance today, and through Mbiti's leadership Bossey began to play an important role in this area.

With the help of the WCC's Programme on Theological Education and other partners Mbiti organized a series of *conferences on intercultural theology*. It drew more, and geographically more, representative participants to Bossey than any earlier series of courses or conferences. In the ecumenical movement of that time, Latin American and black American liberation theologians especially had taken up the dialogue with theologians from Western cultures. The Bossey series started by focussing on a dialogue on community in African religions and Christianity. For a second conference over eighty participants came from all over the world, representing all major Christians confessions. The majority were Africans and Asians and the studies concentrated this time on African and Asian contributions to contemporary theology. The report states: "In June 1976 African and Asian theologians met for the first time in the history of the church... For the church to be truly ecumenical, it must relate to the thinking, concerns and realities of the whole world." While pioneering for the Africa-Asia dialogue the meeting also became an eye-opener for theologians from Europe and the Americas.

The series continued with a colloquium, with some 110 participants on the central theme of *confessing Christ in different cultures*.
This time theologians from Latin America, the Caribbean, North
America, Europe and the Middle East also made their contributions to
the discussion. Bible studies on the Pentecost story brought this
extremely diverse group with its many tensions close together. There
were signs that the one-sided emphasis on contextual theology was
broadening. Some of the discussion groups examined how one may
reach from a contextual to a universal confession of Christ and how
such a confession can find expression in liturgy and worship, subjects
with which the Council's Faith and Order Commission was at that
time greatly concerned. The two following colloquia looked at how
indigenous theology relates to the universal church and on how Christ,
liturgy and culture are intimately inter-related. The series ended with a
meeting on the prophetic witness in cultural contexts. The gospel and
culture theme continued on the Bossey agenda.

Creeds are communicated within cultures not only through words,
but also in celebrations and rites by *signs and symbols*. Western
Protestants often neglect this. Under Blancy's leadership Bossey
organized two meetings on the role played by signs and symbols in the
communication of the gospel. The majority of participants were
professional or amateur communicators in the arts, the media and in
Bible societies, mostly from the Western world. The gatherings
became an action-reflection exercise. Participants were asked to go
and find an object which they felt symbolized their personality. These
symbolic objects were then shared with and commented upon by the
whole group. It led to a series of Bible studies on John 4 and to
theoretical input on the symbolic structure of a human person and
society. More practical workshops dealt with the media of poetry,
painting, audiovisuals, music and mime, and the acts of worship at the
meetings consciously attempted to make use of such diversity of
expression.

Bossey as a guesthouse

From its beginning Bossey functioned also as an ecumenical
conference centre. Occasionally the governing bodies of the World
Council and other Geneva-based ecumenical organizations met there
and held study sessions and training courses. Even in the early years,
outside groups from the region came to Bossey with their own

programme, such as Paul Tournier's group of medical doctors. But there was no strategy to attract groups not directly involved with the Institute's programme. Until the 1970s there was no pressing financial need to encourage the use of the château as a conference centre. This changed with the dollar crisis and the new by-laws.

The development of the guesthouse section had a double purpose. First, it was an attempt to generate more income. Second, it provided an opportunity for groups from the outside "to be involved in the broader ecumenical education through the Institute and the Ecumenical Centre in Geneva". It was hoped that Bossey as a guesthouse could fulfill this double function "without converting its atmosphere into that of a cool streamlined hotel operation". This, however, became a difficult task. The primary work of the Institute, its programme section, had to continue, but the same house, the same staff and the same board were to help with the guesthouse section as well.

In 1978 Ed van der Burgh started his work as the manager of the guesthouse with much enthusiasm and commitment. Better housing and hosting facilities had to be provided. The access road to the château was tarred. In the entry hall a reception desk, telephone booths and other facilities were provided for the guests. To make their stay at Bossey more comfortable, they had to be served better food, and additional facilities for leisure time activities had to be planned. Bossey as a guesthouse had to be publicized and a conscious strategy developed to attract visiting groups and also individual guests. All this cost money, but gradually it brought in more income.

Not all guesthouse projects could be implemented. There never was enough money to make the château fully accessible to physically handicapped persons, although some improvements were made in this respect. The plan to transform the barn at Petit Bossey into a young people's camp did not meet the approval of the board and the programme staff. The proposal to create a camping site on the grounds of the Institute was turned down by the municipality of Bogis-Bossey.

It soon became clear that there were different priorities for the resident ecumenical teaching and learning fellowship in the Graduate School and the Institute's summer courses on the one hand and for a hotel business on the other. Often one or more visiting groups stayed at Bossey while meetings of the Institute's programme section were in session. This could lead to fruitful exchanges, but it also created tensions. Different daily schedules sometimes came into conflict. To hold together the primary work of the Institute and the needs and dynamics of a developing guesthouse section became increasingly difficult.

The number of *visiting groups* increased. In the early 1980s annually more than fifty such groups came to stay for up to one week, the large majority of them from West Germany — pastors, students of theological schools, parish groups. Most of them came with their own programmes and resource persons and Bossey had only to provide board and lodging. For about twenty of these groups Bossey and the Geneva headquarters had to organize a programme of ecumenical education. During five years the guesthouse itself offered each summer a two-week "ecumenical holiday" where individual guests and families could combine vacations with ecumenical learning. Also an experiment was tried with summer workcamps for teenagers, combining voluntary manual work for the Institute with learning about the ecumenical movement.

The guesthouse activities had consequences for the teaching team. During the period between the Graduate Schools there were now fewer ecumenical summer courses and specialized conferences to be prepared than in earlier years. In theory this meant that the teaching staff had more time for study, preparation and follow-up on the primary Bossey programme as well as for organizing extension work in other countries and continents. In practice this was not the case. As most Bossey programme courses were now jointly organized with several WCC sub-units and with other partners, they involved much time-consuming and often frustrating committee work. The visiting groups wanted to meet not only the Bossey house staff and people in Geneva but also the director and the resident lecturers of the Institute. For many lecturers, this meant additional work. Often it simply was not possible to separate neatly the programme section of work from guesthouse activities. The board recognized this fact. In 1984 the position of associate director for administration was discontinued, and this added to the staff problems.

It needs to be emphasized, however, that Bossey as a guesthouse makes its own specific contributions to the ecumenical movement. First of all it helps financially to continue the work of the Institute. No conference centre, theological college or similar institution with a low occupancy rate can survive without heavy subsidies or large endowments. Bossey had neither of these. It could, nevertheless, offer rudimentary ecumenical education to its guests, because of its proximity to international organizations in Geneva and through the resident teaching staff. Many people who would not normally participate in a course or conference of the Institute's programme could this way come by some understanding of the ecumenical movement. A staff group from educational sub-units of the Council explored with the Bossey staff ways of further developing such ecumenical learning through visiting groups. Many of the proposals made proved to be too expensive, both in terms of finance and staff time. From 1982 onwards an arrangement was made with churches in Germany so that each summer a young ministerial candidate, usually a former Graduate School student, could pursue his or her practical in-service training (vicariate) at the Institute and help with the German visiting groups programme.

The weaknesses and ambiguities of guesthouse activities must also be faced. Long experience has shown that ecumenical education is much more than simply providing information about the ecumenical movement. It consists essentially in believers and seekers coming from different confessional and cultural backgrounds living, worshipping and studying together, with a view to becoming part of a common prophetic and priestly presence in the world. With its competent interpreters, its multi-lingual ecumenical library and its multi-cultural and multi-confessional residential staff, Bossey is uniquely equipped to help with such ecumenical teaching and learning. However, if during several months of the year mainly monolingual visiting groups from the same national and confessional background come to Bossey, the facilities which the Institute offers become under-used. It must also be recognized that during the summer months the guesthouse programme strongly accentuates the one-sided European character of the Institute. This is perhaps one of the inevitable limitations which such an Institute, situated in Europe, must accept.

6. Looking towards the Year 2000

"The patient is well, but the patient is also weak." In these words Karl Hertz summed up the situation of Bossey before turning over the leadership of the Institute to his successor. Now there was no further talk about closing Bossey. After the World Council assembly at Vancouver in 1983, a new board, and again a frequently changing teaching staff, were in charge.

In this chapter, lacking the distance from the period that a credible historical survey requires, we can only single out a few points. We shall also examine how the four different agendas which marked the life and work of the Institute throughout its history have made their impact since 1983: the agenda of the staff team, that of the member churches of the World Council, the agenda of biblical faith, and that of the world.

Looking back on the last decade

The first thing to notice is the fact that work did continue, though not by any means as a matter of course. During the last ten or twenty years many church conference centres around the world had to face great difficulties and a number of them were forced to close down. A number of the churches which together form the World Council saw their membership, and consequently also their budgets, declining. Like most international organizations the World Council too went from one financial crisis to another. Major support for the work of Bossey had come from Germany, the USA and Switzerland, and in these countries churches and ecumenical organizations faced a situation of dwindling resources and public influence. No wonder that during the whole of the last decade considerations of finance lay behind many decisions taken with regard to Bossey. Nevertheless, the work continued, in the first place the Graduate School and the guesthouse activities, and to a lesser degree in ecumenical education summer courses and some frontier work. This was possible only through the devotion of a hard-working staff in both the guest-house and the programme section.

The situation implied a *certain loss of freedom* for pioneering work by the Institute. During the last few years almost all meetings at Bossey were sponsored, prepared and conducted jointly by the Institute's staff, the sub-units of the World Council, and partner organizations such as the world confessional families. This helped to avoid the danger of too little coordination between the work initiated at Bossey and the WCC headquarters. Now the subjects taken up in summer courses and the themes of the Graduate Schools clearly reflect work already initiated and pursued by other ecumenical agencies to which Bossey makes a contribution of its own. This trend worried several members of the board which, after Vancouver, was chaired by Milan Opocensky. The question was raised whether Bossey "should not take up more of a pioneer role, exploring themes that have not yet been taken up by the WCC and anticipating discussions that will take place. A critical, corrective role was more fitting for Bossey programmes than just following the slogans of the WCC. Bossey had to be primarily in the service of the churches and not of the World Council." Slogans were developed at the Institute also, and the Bossey label is no guarantee of excellence. Nevertheless, such opinions were several times voiced in the 1980s.

The last decade has been strongly marked by *the collaboration between Bossey and the Programme on Theological Education*. This meant that educational questions, ecumenical learning, training for ministry and the role of theology received a large place in the Institute's programme. The ecumenical concern for theological education began with the International Missionary Council and it was a two-million dollar grant from John D. Rockefeller, Jr, which made possible in 1958 the launching of the Theological Education Fund. Bossey and this Fund thus had the same financial ancestry. The Fund concentrated first on helping to develop theological education in former missionary areas, but gradually broadened its scope. In 1977 it became the Programme on Theological Education (PTE) and its offices were moved from London to Geneva. Even at that time a closer cooperation between Bossey and that programme was envisaged. Within PTE much creative thinking had developed on contextual theology, on "theology by the people" and on innovative forms of training for the ministry — all of them subjects closely related to what had been taking place at the Ecumenical Institute since the 1950s. An increasing cooperation between these two partners appeared to hold out fresh possibilities.

The governing bodies of the World Council therefore decided in 1989 to initiate an arranged marriage. Several members of the Bossey board and of the PTE commission expressed serious doubts about the wisdom of such a full merger, though on paper it looked promising. By pooling the resources the proposed Ecumenical Theological Education work unit would have a strong, representative staff team who could bring together residential work (the former Bossey programme) and global work (the former PTE travels and projects). Both Bossey's desire to do extension work and PTE's wish to have a place for teaching would thus be realized. The merger took place in 1990. What made it specially attractive was the fact that it meant considerable saving; now two programmes could be managed with one director and a single supervisory body. But it soon appeared that this arranged marriage might not work. Global work through staff visitations in different continents needed a certain continuity. Residential work at the Institute needed the permanent presence of a teaching team with the learning communities and the house staff. Neither of the two different tasks could be done on a part-time basis. Moreover, the advisory committee for Ecumenical Theological Education could not replace the important work of the former Bossey board. In 1993 once again a review committee was asked to examine yet again the future of the Institute. In 1995 both Bossey and the PTE regained their separate identities and their own supervising and advisory boards, while fruitful collaboration in areas of common concern was to continue.

During the last decade some important developments have taken place in *guest-house activities*. There is no longer any strict separation between the guest-house and programme sections. All the staff are involved in both. Fruitful collaboration between Bossey and the World Council headquarters has been developed for organizing the visitors' programmes. We have already discussed the special contributions and ambiguities of the work with outside groups (see pp.112-13). Groups from Germany still predominate, but groups from other countries come as well, from the USA, Denmark and even from Korea. Some secular international organizations, such as the World Wildlife Foundation, have begun to use Bossey facilities. Statistics for 1993-94 show that during these two years 66 groups, with an average strength of 24 in each, came for a week's stay with their own programmes while Bossey organized ecumenical education programmes for 34 additional outside groups. This of course does not include some 2500 visitors who came for just a day's stay.

The present major programme activity of Bossey, the *Graduate School*, has continued with an average student strength of fifty to sixty, recruited from all continents and confessions. The themes taken up were related to ongoing World Council studies or to themes of World Council assemblies and conferences. In response to student criticism and to new thinking about ecumenical education some changes were made in the schedules of the last few semesters. For instance:

— Some blocks of programme work concentrate during a whole week on one single concern. Thus the first week is devoted to conscious community-building, with special training in cultural and gender sensitivity. Another week early in the semester deals with questions of worship in an ecumenical setting. Yet another takes up Orthodox theology and spirituality. In some semesters a week is mainly devoted to ecumenical Bible studies.

— Such a schedule means that less time is now available for a serious and unhurried study of the semester's main theme (see appendix A). Several times the board discussed whether the theme approach should not be replaced by a more structured curriculum of ecumenical studies. To take up a large theme and to combine the study of it with Bossey's stated purpose of learning about ecumenical history and present World Council work is to attempt the impossible.

— Participants' input happens mainly in the seminar groups. Besides papers written during the semester, each student is now asked to prepare, before coming to Bossey, a short paper on the theme as seen from his or her own background. Seminar work then starts with the presentation and discussion of these papers.

— The period after the Christmas vacation was often difficult and unsatisfactory. The staff and the new board therefore decided that for a trial period from 1996 onwards the Graduate School should be shortened, and scheduled from September to December.

An important development of the last decade was the *strengthening of the links between Bossey and various nearby local churches.* The circle of "Friends of Bossey" has been created. During the

Graduate School, specially prepared Bible studies on the semester theme are held in homes, attended by students and members of the local churches. Bossey's neighbours thus become interested in the work of the Institute. Some of them have supported the recent restoration of the château and the buildings at Petit Bossey.

The last decade has also been marked by the effort to renew contact with *former participants of Bossey meetings*. In 1986 on the occasion of the 40th anniversary of the Institute, an attempt was made to write to all former Graduate School students whose addresses were available. In connection with the Jubilee in 1996 a more systematic effort is being made. This time it is not simply an invitation to remember the Institute and to provide financial support; an important concern is to solicit contributions to the Bossey Endowment Fund. The new attempt to strengthen links with former participants also focuses on initiating a worldwide reflection on ecumenical education. In several countries work on this has already started.

With regard to programme, the last decade has seen the *presence and influence of more women*. Bossey cannot claim to have been a pioneer in this field. Secular women's organizations, the World's YWCA and the World Student Christian Federation were the pioneers. After Suzanne de Diétrich left the staff in 1954, it took more than thirty years to appoint a woman on the Institute's resident teaching staff. Yet from 1984 onwards almost every year Bossey had one or two meetings that focused on various aspects of women's life experiences and women's contributions to church and society. Evident in all the following four agenda areas of work is this growing presence of women.

The agenda of the staff

Through the participants at the Institute's meetings Bossey is continually evolving. Yet a measure of continuity is maintained by the long-term staff, those who bridge the period from one director to another. A faithful group from earlier periods continued serving Bossey during the whole or most of the last decade: the librarian Margret Koch; the interpreters Margaret Pater, Roswitha Ginglas and Evelyne Tatu; Sheila Ray and her colleagues in the office; the *gouvernante* Marianne Dessoulavy and the burser John McVie who supervised the restoration of the château's exterior. Several of those who cook and clean also belong to this faithful group of staff. New, equally devoted members of the support staff have joined the team, for example in the key position for reception and hospitality the coordinator Brigitte Guichard. She aptly described the experience of the long-term staff when she said: *"Nous sommes comme des nomades sur place"* — nomads who stay in the same place, but a place that is ever-changing with all the coming and going of groups. Besides the long-term staff members the group of blue angels continue to be a part of daily life at Bossey. After several years, the presence once again of two sisters from Grandchamp during part of the Graduate School enriches the Institute's worship and community.

The two persons who made the bridge in the teaching team from one period to another were Hans Goedeking and Dan-Ilie Ciobotea, who were both introduced in the last chapter. Also John Lucal still lived at Bossey while working at Geneva. Leaving for high ecclesiastical duties in the Romanian Orthodox Church after serving on the teaching team for eight years, Ciobotea sums up what Bossey has remained in the 1980s as well: "An institute for ecumenical dialogue and spirituality rather than an institute for ecumenical research producing studies and books... A place of freedom where the hearts of strangers are often converted to ecumenical friendship."

The new director, the Dutch Reformed theologian *Adriaan Geense*, had been a student of the 7th Graduate School and he knew the strengths and weaknesses of Bossey from the inside. He was a world-open Barthian, tempered with Dutch humour. In any case, it was the older Barth that he followed, the wiser dogmatician who spoke about the humanity of God and wrote that with the growth of churches in continents and cultures outside the Western world all the confessions which grew up in the ancient church and the Reformation have become "a European affair". Geense had worked as student pastor in Germany and a professor of systematic theology at Groningen university in the Netherlands. He came to Bossey not with a closed system of dogmatics but with a great openness to thinking theologically. In the Graduate Schools and the summer courses he stimulated much biblically based reflection on the challenges to Christian faith in the changing European situation, in the dialogue with people of other living faiths and in the modern search for human identity. As director Geense had to reorganize staff responsibilities so that the activities of the guest-house and the Bossey programme were again better integrated. He and his wife, Anneke Geense-Ravestein, attempted to work as a team and she shared with him responsibility for several summer courses.

Geense took up the chair of systematic theology in Geneva university in 1989. Plans to merge Bossey with the Programme for Theological Education were by then in an advanced stage. Thus *Samuel Amirtham*, the director of that programme, took over, on a half-time basis, the directorship of Bossey. This Old Testament teacher from India was aware of developments in theological education around the world. He also had inside knowledge of life and work at Bossey because he lived on the campus and had served as a member of the board. His term lasted less than a year as he was called back to India to serve as a bishop of the Church of South India.

The present director, *Jacques Nicole*, has brought to Bossey a rich experience of transcultural life and theology. After working as a youth pastor in French-speaking Switzerland and serving a local church in the Alps of the Canton of Vaud, he was for 15 years in the South Pacific. There for a time he taught biblical theology at the theological school in Tahiti, and later became associate director and Old Testament teacher at the Pacific Theological College in Suva, Fiji. He had just published the findings of an interdisciplinary research on the translation of the Bible into Tahitian with all the linguistic, sociological and religious questions involved in such a transcultural effort. Nicole was called to become the director of the Ecumenical Theological Education sub-unit and he struggled hard to make this arranged marriage between PTE and Bossey work. His genial nature and his many links with French-speaking Switzerland gave the Institute more rooting in its geographic environment. Thanks to his efforts the château again has a roof that does not leak and has been made presentable for the Jubilee celebrations of the Institute in October 1996.

In order to correct the disproportionate European composition of the Bossey teaching staff, *tutors from other continents* were employed to help with the Graduate School, a number of them seconded by partners from outside. Others were paid out of the Bossey scholarship fund — which meant that by 1990 this fund for students had become considerably depleted.

In 1985 once again an Asian joined the resident staff team. *Cyris Moon*, an Old Testament professor from the Presbyterian seminary in

Seoul, worked at Bossey for five years. He had earlier been a tutor at the Graduate School, and he introduced Bossey to the Korean minjung theology, a reading of the Bible and a theological reflection coming out of the suffering and struggles of common Korean people. Moon had special responsibilities for Bossey extension work which now was called "Bossey in partnership". In 1986 and 1987 the whole teaching staff of the Institute went for visitations and ecumenical seminars to Romania and to Cuba.

In the mid-1980s, there was at long last *a woman's presence* on the teaching staff — *Ofelia Ortega* from Cuba, a participant of the 16th Graduate School, pastor of the Cuban Presbyterian Church and professor of Christian education. She brought with her the warm Caribbean temperament, the strength of basic Christian communities and the concern that women's experiences and contributions be heard and recognized in the ecumenical movement. After two years she joined the staff of the PTE, but she continued to live at Bossey and contribute much to women's seminars.

The person who has carried on and developed since 1991 Bossey's concern for the contribution of women's life experiences and theology is *Beate Stierle*, a German Lutheran minister who specialized in church history. She worked as a pastor and study director at a training centre for ministerial candidates after their academic studies. In the course of the last few years she has developed a major concern for bringing together various kinds of feminist theologies that are developing in different confessions and continents.

After Nissiotis and Ciobotea, the Orthodox presence at Bossey continued in quite a new way with *K.M. George*, priest and theologian from the ancient Syrian Orthodox Church in South India. He had served as a board member since the Vancouver assembly. During his five-year service George's major contribution to the life and work at Bossey was a remarkable combination of Asian and Orthodox spirituality. This expressed itself through the family life of K.M. and Mariam as well, and it was a delight to have their young children on the campus. George saw to it that in the Orthodox seminars and on other teaching occasions the Oriental Orthodox traditions and liturgies were not ignored. The most recent member of the Bossey teaching team is *Athanasios Hatzopoulos*, a Greek Orthodox monk and theologian, who joined the Institute in 1994.

Year after year *the Roman Catholic presence* at Bossey had continued through tutors and visiting lecturers, sponsored first by Fribourg university and then by the Vatican Secretariat for Promoting Christian Unity. In 1989, for the first time in Bossey's history, a Roman Catholic priest and theologian joined the resident teaching team for a seven-year term. *Francis Frost* from Great Britain was seconded by what has now become the Pontifical Council for Promoting Christian Unity. He has special interests in interconfessional dialogue, notably with Methodist churches, and a great concern to link academic studies with worship. He was also much involved in the joint consultations of the Christian Medical Commission and Bossey. A Roman Catholic priest and biblical scholar from East Africa will take his place in 1996.

It must be noted that during *the period from 1990 to 1993* all members of the teaching staff at Bossey also worked half-time for theological education programmes around the world, and all members of the PTE staff worked the same way for Bossey. This was the case with Ofelia Ortega who had become PTE secretary for Latin America and the Caribbean, Judo Poerwowidagdo, an Indonesian theologian and PTE Asia/Pacific secretary, and John Pobee, a Ghanaian theologian and PTE secretary for Africa, at present director of PTE. Pobee was the main leader at the 40th Graduate School.

What have been the common features and *common agenda points* in this teaching team since 1983? There obviously — and fortunately — was a great diversity of confessional and cultural backgrounds, of gifts, interests and competences. All of them were theologians by training; most of them had been involved in theological teaching, especially in the fields of systematic theology, biblical theology and Christian education. None of them had come out of a long-time secular employment in the present-day world. This has undoubtedly shaped the main emphases of the programme of Bossey during the most recent period in its history.

When in 1995 Bossey again became a work unit on its own, a *new board* was appointed, moderated by Robert Welsh, a former Graduate School participant and a staff member of the American Disciples of Christ Church which in the Institute's history has played a continuous supporting role. The staff team can once again count on the concern, expertise and friendship of a committed group of lay people, theologians and church administrators.

The agenda of the churches

Bossey-church relationship is of two kinds. The concerns, needs and insights of churches all over the world reach Bossey through the headquarters of the World Council, its governing bodies and its itinerant staff. The Council links many different networks — that of the agencies for interchurch aid, refugee service and development projects, of missionary departments, of action groups in many of the struggles of society, of ecumenical study committees and of church headquarters in all continents. Church leaders form the great majority of the Council's governing body. What reaches Bossey from the churches through the Council is a global picture, mediated and interpreted. Bossey also has a more direct, personalized and obviously more random contact with churches through the people who come to meetings. In a very direct way some of the sufferings and hopes, failures and achievements in many local churches and Christian groups from around the world thus become part of Bossey's experience, especially during the Graduate School.

How has this double relationship between the Institute and the churches functioned during the last decade? Two tendencies may be observed. Probably more than ever the programme was shaped by what the World Council discerned as important issues of the churches. Since the mid-1970s one or more headquarters staff committees, together with Bossey staff, have tried to make sure that the work done at the Institute was related to the work done by the Council. Clearly the first kind of Bossey-church relationships had predominated. At the same time, never in its history had the Institute had more direct contact with local church life, not only with parishes in the region and through the visiting groups from other places, but also through the present concerted effort to re-establish a closer relationship with former participants. In the future this can have an important impact on the Bossey programme and can strengthen its pioneering role.

Issues of *church life in different confessions and continents* remained on the Institute's programme. The Orthodox seminar took place annually, though in recent years it has been held every other year in an Orthodox country, as it was in Romania and Greece. Twice Bossey meetings were devoted to new developments in the Roman Catholic Church. Twice the legacy of Calvinism and the Geneva Reformation were chosen as subjects. Special conferences dealt with church life in North America, Asia, Africa and Europe. All these were done in collaboration with the Council staff in Geneva and other partners.

A series of courses on the Faith and Order statement on *baptism, eucharist and ministry* was conducted in order to introduce theological students, pastors/priests and lay people to these studies. This convergence statement led to a meeting which examined what convergence in theology means for congregational renewal. The study on the eucharist was followed by a workshop on the Lima liturgy, a proposed eucharistic service which arose out of the Faith and Order studies. With so many theological educators present in the Bossey team the statement on ministry obviously received much attention. What are its implications for the training of ministers? What about the ministry of women and of women theological teachers? Is not ministry in the Faith and Order statement seen in a narrow and overly church-centred way? Bossey therefore complemented the series of courses on baptism, eucharist and ministry with a course on the ministry of the laity and with a meeting examining the whole spectrum of ministry.

The main emphasis of Bossey in its early years, *the ministry of the laity in the world*, was thus not ignored during the last decade, but it was mainly examined from the point of view of theological education and from the perspective of the gathered church. As J.H. Oldham had recognized, the role of the laity is differently understood if looked at from the perspective of the scattered church, from the point of view of Christians gaining their livelihood in secular professions. In recent years Bossey has developed new contacts with lay training centres and held a few frontier conferences. All this might influence the Institute's programme in the future.

The *stronger presence of women* is already beginning to have an impact. At the 41st Graduate School, for the first time as many women participated as men. Within the temporary house church which comes into being with every semester at Bossey the women's presence has shaped the whole style of community life, making it more welcoming and caring. In the series of women's seminars several were specifically devoted to such contributions of women in church life. Stereotypes of the women's ministry were challenged, and new models of community life and new ways of church leadership were explored. A workshop was held on inclusive liturgy and music. It is significant that the reports of these seminars contain more poetry and stories than conference reports normally do.

The most innovative seminars in this series brought together representatives of *feminist and Orthodox spiritualities*. One would not normally expect these two groups to enter into a fruitful dialogue. The first meeting was a timid attempt to get to know one another. But having built up a measure of trust, the second meeting was a time of mutual challenging and learning. Through common study and sensitive listening to one another and through moments of crisis and common worship the participants discovered they had similar problems, and were able to grow in understanding.

Several conferences and courses of the last decade dealt with the *ecumenical perspective on the churches' life and mission*. There were meetings on teaching ecumenics and on ecumenical leadership formation. But what does "ecumenical" mean? Neither the ecumenical movement at large nor the governing bodies of the World Council, neither the headquarters staff nor the Bossey board and teaching team can give a common answer to that question. The Institute must therefore work with an open mind and different understandings of what "ecumenical" means. All talk about ecumenical education or ecumenical learning becomes frustrating unless this dilemma is recognized and faced.

Among the *different understandings of the term "ecumenical"* the following four must receive serious attention:
— For a first group "ecumenical" points almost exclusively to church unity and has primarily to do with interconfessional dialogue. The Decree on Ecumenism of the Second Vatican Council uses the term in this traditional sense. It defines the ecumenical movement as comprising all activities and enterprises "for the fostering of unity among Christians".
— A second group, while placing church unity at the centre, expands the concern for unity to the unity of humankind. Here also the mission and service of the churches and the renewal of their life are taken as an integral part of the ecumenical movement. Typical of this understanding is the statement on "Ecumenical Formation", formulated by the Joint Working Group between the Roman Catholic Church and the WCC and published in 1993. It starts with the imperative for church unity and ends with the new heaven and the new earth.
— A third group understands the meaning of "ecumenical" in the light of what actually develops within that trend in modern church

history since the late 19th century which is generally called "the ecumenical movement". This trend led to such organizations as the World Student Christian Federation and the World Council of Churches and it also strongly marked such events as the Second Vatican Council. For this group it is not right to put just one concern at the centre, be it unity, mission or renewal. The original statement of the "basis" of the WCC had to be changed and expanded in 1961 because the ecumenical movement which the Council wanted to serve had meanwhile developed and expanded. Similarly, the understanding of what is meant by "ecumenical" cannot be dogmatically fixed once and for all.

— A fourth group works with a much wider concept of "ecumenical", designating by it the encounter and community of all the world's cultures and living faiths.

What is, in the light of its history, *Bossey's understanding of "ecumenical"*? Clearly, neither the first nor the last of these understandings has figured prominently in it.

— Church unity was of course considered important and the prayer for unity has been offered unceasingly in the chapel of Bossey. Several summer courses and conferences and a few semesters of the Graduate School were specially devoted to the theme of unity. Nevertheless, church unity was not the one central thrust. At the Institute the Vatican Council's Dogmatic Constitution on Divine Revelation and the pastoral constitution on the Church in the Modern World were considered as more important ecumenical documents than the Decree on Ecumenism.

— Dialogue with people of other living faiths and dialogue among people from different cultures were increasingly seen as important in the Bossey programme. Nevertheless, such dialogues were not conducted from a neutral, outsider's point of view but from the perspective of the Christian faith.

— In Bossey's life and work the second and, even more, the third of the above-mentioned understandings of "ecumenical" have been operative.

The different understandings of what the ecumenical movement was, is, and is becoming explain *Bossey's dilemma with regard to ecumenical research institutes.* In 1978 the European Societas Oecumenica was founded, interlinking Protestant, Roman Catholic and Orthodox research institutes and professors of ecumenics. Several times Bossey was asked to relate more actively to teachers of ecumenics and ecumenical research institutes. The plan to transform the barn at Petit Bossey into such a research institute with resident scholars had been revived, and Bossey was challenged to become a "think tank" for the World Council. There is no doubt that ecumenical research should be promoted. Because of its official relationship with the university in Geneva Bossey can help with such research if it can secure the necessary funds. Should such old plans for a research institute in relation with the Graduate School finally be realized, Bossey would have to make sure that ecumenical research is not undertaken with too narrow an understanding of what "ecumenical" means.

The agenda of biblical faith

The readiness to be constantly corrected, guided and encouraged by *a message and force from beyond* human time and space is what gives the ecumenical movement, the churches, the World Council and Bossey their specific character. Christians confess that this voice and action come from God, the father of Abraham, Isaac and Jacob, the God of Sarah, Rebekah and Ruth, the One who visited us in Jesus Christ and who renews the creation by the power of the Spirit. Confessions of this biblical faith are only feeble and stumbling responses to the divine reality from beyond. Therefore these responses of faith must constantly be nourished by corporate listening to the message from beyond and by a re-formation of our life of obedience. This has happened at Bossey.

Gospel and culture was perhaps the foremost agenda point imposed by biblical faith on Bossey in the last decade. Two semesters of the Graduate School and several summer courses dealt with this theme, which became also the subject of a colloquium during the 40th anniversary year of the Institute. Two factors led to the concentration on this theme.

— First, all creeds are marked by the period of time, language and culture in which they were formulated. Yet faith needs to be rethought again and again for the present time. To stimulate such rethinking Bossey organized a meeting on the ecumenical significance of the Barmen Declaration of 1934 by which the Confessing Church in Germany witnessed to Jesus Christ in the context of growing Nazi ideology.

— Second, each creed is marked also by the geographic area in which and for which Christian faith is confessed. In ecumenical encounters it becomes apparent how strongly the ancient creeds of the Eastern and Western church are marked by the old Mediterranean world and how strongly the Reformation confessions (and the Barmen declaration) are marked by European history and European thought patterns. Therefore meetings were organized on confessing Christ in Asia and in Africa. The dialogue of theologies, started at Bossey in the 1970s, has continued.

Not only are new formulations of biblical faith needed, but also reflections on *ways of confessing faith.* What role does popular religiosity play in the communication of the gospel? How is faith expressed through visual arts and through music? Can modern mass media become vehicles for confessing the biblical faith? In collaboration with partners Bossey organized meetings on such subjects. Recently, for instance, a seminar examined what can be learned from the way black Americans express the Christian faith by "singing the Lord's song in a strange land".

Since 1984, a symbol of the concern for cultural rootedness has been a part of the Bossey campus — the fifteen-metre high *totem pole* that stands close to the entrance to the lecture hall. It was carved by Canadian Indian prisoners and presented as a gift to the Vancouver World Council assembly. Those who worked on it explained that the pole represents "humanity's spiritual search through the ages, the story of the people who follow the spirit of God". At the bottom the creation story as transmitted by Canadian Indians is visually told. The eagle and thunderbird at the top represent the spiritual stage at which humankind begins to see "that a force greater than anything on earth controls all". This is not a confession of the New Testament faith, but the pole communicates the understanding of life and the genuine spiritual search of an oppressed people struggling for identity and for regaining the land of which they were robbed. In the context of such living faiths the gospel-culture study has much to contribute, and it is significant that the pole now stands on Bossey ground.

Confessing biblical faith calls for *the discipline of Bible study.* During the last decades the Bossey programme included two training courses for Bible-study enablers, taking up a tradition of earlier times. Special attention was given to the different ways and the different media through which, in the Bible itself, faith traditions are transmitted and confessed and what this implies for present-day biblical interpretation and for ecumenical Bible study. The major biblical consultation of this last period was one dealing with biblical and theological perspectives on power. The Bossey tradition of reading of Bible together with Jews was continued in a recent symposium that explored the biblical institution and vision of the Jubilee Year and its significance for today.

The series of women's consultations, sponsored by several partners, included a seminar on *reading the Bible with women's eyes*. It attempted to develop a more inclusive interpretation of biblical texts and themes for our time than are found in most commentaries written by male scholars and sermons preached by male preachers. At least as important as the new theories about feminist biblical interpretation are the many concrete examples of Bible studies animated during the seminars by women from different continents, where texts are seen and understood in the context of women's experiences of life.

The test of Christian discipleship comes in periods of pain, when people cry out to God, as Korean minjung theologians have shown. *Suffering and faith* belong together. Experiencing God in suffering and hope was the theme of the 24th Graduate School. More recently also this relationship of faith with suffering and healing was taken up.

During the early years of Bossey there was a strong concentration on God's saving work through Christ's redeeming ministry. As generally in World Council studies, so also here more emphasis is now laid on *God's creating and sanctifying work.* This has led to a reflection on how to safeguard creation and on God's action through the Spirit in the community of the churches and the renewing of creation. Recent semesters of the Graduate School and Bossey conferences have taken part in this reflection.

The agenda of the world

God's first love is the cosmos. This recalling of Bossey's history would betray both biblical faith and the vision which inspired the creation of the Ecumenical Institute if it were to conclude with the life and faith of the churches. The biblical canon neither begins nor ends with the people of Israel and the churches. It starts with the creation of this cosmos and concludes with the vision of the new heaven and the new earth, that last great parable of God's kingdom. A passion for the world in between this old and the coming new cosmos is at the heart of the ecumenical movement. It must continue to mark the work at Bossey. Sensitivity to the world's agenda means attention to what is actually happening in the world today.

Many observers have noted that people, nations and the whole earth are caught up in *an uncontrollable process of acceleration*. Does it race towards progress or disaster? Opinions and forecasts differ. Acceleration in present history comes probably less from totally new scientific discoveries than from the continuing and increasingly sophisticated technological applications of former discoveries. Even on a lonely atoll of Micronesia the events, ideas and degradations of the globe are now propagated through satellite communication and video-cassettes. Seen from a world perspective Internet is still the medium of a few, but many are convinced that such instant communications will change the world.

Those who profit most from this acceleration are the *economic powers* who compete for the world's markets, and are concentrated in the technologically advanced areas in East Asia, North America and Western Europe. They control a large part of the mass media and use them for selling consumer goods. People are thus seduced into buying ever "new" products, and systematically conditioned by the values of the market. The vast majority of the world's population in the developing countries and the increasing number of unemployed people in the industrialized nations are left with a nagging sense of restlessness, being deprived and marginalized.

In *politics* the period since 1983 witnessed the disintegration of the Soviet bloc, the opening up of China, the erosion of state authority in many countries and the rise of ethnic and religious nationalisms. There have been surprisingly hopeful developments like the relatively non-violent change from a racist minority rule to an inter-racial democracy in South Africa. There have also been terrible developments, such as the break-up of Yugoslavia and the nightmare of ethnic cleansing, and the genocides in Africa. Unlike in the cold-war period, world peace is not under threat, but the climate of conflict and aggression continues, leading to local wars and violence within families and communities.

An ill-defined *feeling of insecurity* is growing through ecological catastrophes like the Chernobyl disaster and through the appearance of illnesses for which there is no cure as yet. Some prophesy that the next world crisis will be a war the earth will wage against humankind in response to the way human beings have been treating the earth, polluting the air, water and land. Are the religious fanaticisms of our time a response to this situation?

A recent debate on French television highlighting *the challenges of the year 2000* illustrated the uncertainty of all forecasts. With a few exceptions the scientists and technologists present spoke enthusiastically about the rapid progress in molecular biology, space research and communication technologies which could change and improve life on the planet earth. The historians and philosophers spoke less positively, and at times very pessimistically about the world's future. When finally two women from poverty-stricken areas in Asia and Latin America joined the debate their contributions had both another ring and another content, very different from those of the scientists and philosophers. Fully involved in local situations, living not in virtual but real reality, they spoke about the struggle for basic health care, against oppressive social and economic structures in their areas and for the healing and growth of human relationships. They spoke with confidence and hope.

For responding to today's world agenda Bossey will have to listen to *contradictory voices*, to scientists and philosophers, to women and men involved in struggles of faith in the structures of this world, to youth and children — who were not part of the French TV discussion. For the Bossey staff it means, in the first place, listening to the voices of the world which come to the Institute through the participants. The opening China comes to Bossey through the mature Chinese representatives who now form part of the student body of Graduate Schools. The new East Europe comes with its broken hopes and critical questions through participants from that region. The suffering Africa came, for example, in the persons of two participants from Rwanda in recent semesters: one a pastor whose wife and children had just been murdered; the other a medical doctor who saw her husband, a member of another ethnic group, being assassinated by members of her own ethnic group. With such participants the carefully prepared programmes of the teaching staff and the planned discussions on ecclesiastical matters have often to be set aside, in order to deal with the immediate crucial issues of this world's agenda.

The acceleration in world history calls for fundamental *reflection on the course of history*. Through the earlier interdisciplinary conferences, for instance on the meaning of history and the process of secularization, Bossey had been successful in stimulating reflection that led to new insights. Perhaps such all-embracing interdisciplinary encounters are impossible today. Nevertheless, during this last decade too the challenge to reflect on the world's destiny was taken up. When George Orwell's fateful year 1984 had gone by, a seminar was convened for philosophers, scientists and theologians on "The Other Side of 1984". Bossey also contributed to the World Council study on "Justice, Peace and the Integrity of Creation" by making it the theme of the 37th Graduate School and through a seminar on science and the theology of creation.

The *relationship between economy, ecology and ethics* was taken up in various seminars and in semesters of the Graduate School. This happened most thoroughly during meetings which the Visser 't Hooft Endowment Fund organized at Bossey with the Institute's collaboration. This Fund was established to make available new resources for developing ecumenical leadership by sponsoring "interdisciplinary research upon crucial world issues confronting the churches today". Its long term aim is to "sponsor a Visser 't Hooft chair at the Ecumenical Institute which will be devoted to research and teaching in this area". Unfortunately, as was the case with Bossey's own endowment fund, the project has not been very successful. Nevertheless, so far two interdisciplinary consultations have been held, one on sustainable growth after the United Nations' earth summit in Rio de Janeiro, and the other on work in a sustainable society.

Another special emphasis of the Institute with regard to the world's agenda concerns the role of *women in today's society*. What do they experience in the midst of the world's violence and what have they to contribute in response to the world's longing for a fuller life? It was one of the recent women's seminars which in the most direct way took up the challenge of the year 2000 and attempted to develop a vision towards the 21st century.

* * *

What does the future hold for the Ecumenical Institute? Readers will have to give their own answers. This story can best be concluded with a quotation from one who had deep insights about Bossey's day-to-day role and its overall vocation, and whose life journey ended too early. Adriaan Geense said in his last report to the board:

Everybody who has had the privilege to live and work in Bossey will have made the same basic experience of both the uniqueness and the fragility of that place. The uniqueness is its situation, the beauty of the place, the space around it, the contacts with "Geneva". It is a space that invites the participants to open themselves to one another, to make the discovery of the richness of the gifts that God bestows on us in the encounter with those who are so different from us.

But Bossey is also a fragile, vulnerable place. All conflicts that arise out of the encounter of cultures arise here as well; the place is not protected; all the imperfections of the participants and the staff are revealed very clearly if one lives so closely together as we do in Bossey. Bossey is also what we bring to it. It has a chapel but no spirituality of its own. It has its organization, but no monastic rules, no prescribed code of behaviour. Its continuity has to be built up every time again: the tears at the departure are as strong a reality as the smile of the first encounter. Participants come and go and staff come and go. Nobody "owns" Bossey. But those who have lived and worked here know that Bossey owns us: that we cannot imagine any other future work where the fact of having been in Bossey has not marked us decisively and been a privilege for which we can never be grateful enough.

Bossey has the power to survive, to survive the changes of time, the crises of history, the departure of its participants and the discontinuity of its staff. It is my hope that this conviction may also inspire many to fulfil their work in faith and with joy, in the atmosphere of responsibility and friendship.

Appendix A:
Graduate School Themes

1st	1952-53	No central theme
2nd	1953-54	Various issues from the areas of
3rd	1954-55	Faith and Order, Church and Society
4th	1955-56	and Mission and Evangelism
5th	1956-57	
6th	1957-58	Strong emphasis on confessional studies
7th	1958-59	"The Roman Catholic World"
8th	1959-60	"The Ministry and the Ministries of the Church"
9th	1960-61	"The Witness of the Church in a Non-Christian and Post-Christian World"
10th	1961-62	"Man in the Light of Christ"
11th	1962-63	"Worship and Daily Life"
12th	1963-64	"Syncretism"
13th	1964-65	"The Church and the People of Israel"
14th	1965-66	"The Church in a Technological World"
15th	1966-67	"The Ecumenical Movement after the Second Vatican Council"
16th	1967-68	"Renewal in the World and the Church"
17th	1968-69	"Evangelism"
18th	1969-70	"The Future of the Church"
19th	1970-71	"The Bible: Contesting and Contested"
20th	1971-72	"Participation in Change"
21st	1972-73	"Dialogue on Salvation with People of Living Faiths and Ideologies"
22nd	1973-74	"God's Action in a World Planned by Man"
23rd	1974-75	"Jesus Christ Frees and Unites"
24th	1975-76	"Experiencing God in Suffering and Hope"
25th	1976-77	"Who Do You Say that I Am?"
26th	1977-78	"Church, State and Power"
27th	1978-79	"The Holy Spirit and the Ministry of the Church"
28th	1979-80	"The Kingdom of God and the Future of Humanity"

29th	1980-81	"The Bible in the Life of the Church"
30th	1981-82	"Created in the Image and Likeness of God"
31st	1982-83	"Jesus Christ, the Life of the World"
32nd	1983-84	"The Visible Unity of the Church in a Divided World"
33rd	1984-85	"Faith and Christian Discipleship Today"
34th	1985-86	"Gospel and Culture" I
35th	1986-87	"Gospel and Culture" II
36th	1987-88	"Unity and Mission of the Church"
37th	1988-89	"Justice, Peace and the Integrity of the Creation"
38th	1989-90	"The Holy Spirit and the Prophetic Witness of the Church"
39th	1990-91	"Come, Holy Spirit — Renew the Whole Creation"
40th	1991-92	"Towards New Models of Communities"
41st	1992-93	"Towards an Inclusive Community"
42nd	1993-94	"Towards Communion in Faith, Life and Witness"
43rd	1994-95	"Education for Koinonia"
44th	1995-96	"Theology for Life"

Appendix B:
Staff

Directors and teaching team

1946-55:	**Hendrik Kraemer**
1946-54:	Suzanne de Dietrich
1946-51:	Henry-Louis Henriod
1949-54:	Hans-Hermann Walz
1954-58:	Robert S. Paul
1955-66:	**Hans-Heinrich Wolf**
1956-61:	Charles C. West
1958-74:	**Nikos Nissiotis**
1960-64:	Henry Makulu
1961-71:	Hans-Ruedi Weber
1964-67:	Samuel L. Parmar
1966-69:	Joseph C. Weber
1967-70:	Anwar Barkat
1969-72:	Michael Keeling
1971-81:	Alain Blancy
1972-73:	Gert von Wahlert
1972-76:	Rihito Kimura
1974-76:	Johannes Panagopoulos
1974-80:	**John Mbiti**
1976-84:	Hans Goedeking
1978-83:	**Karl H. Hertz**
1980-88:	Dan-Ilie Ciobotea
1983-89:	**Adriaan Geense**
1985-88:	Ofelia Ortega
1985-90:	Cyris Moon
1989-90:	**Samuel Amirtham**
1989-94:	K.M. George
1989-96:	Francis Frost
1989-	**Jacques Nicole**

| 1991- | Beate Stierle |
| 1994- | Athanasios Hatzopoulos |

Long-term staff

1948-61:	Ilse Friedeberg
1948-73:	Simone Mathil
1955-66:	Renée Béguin
1957-77:	Herman de Graaf
1963-66 and 1975-89:	Margaret Pater
1963-70:	Dorli Kimmel
1966-73:	Bärbel Fischer
1966-94:	Margret Koch
1968-76:	Eva-Maria Schneck
1973-	Roswitha Ginglas
1973-	Evelyne Tatu
1977-	Sheila Ray
1977-94:	John McVie
1978-83:	Ed van der Burgh
1981-89:	Marianne Dessoulavy
1990-	Brigitte Guichard

Appendix C:
Bibliography

History of Bossey

The archives at Bossey contain directors' reports and minutes of board meetings; correspondence; course programmes and lists of participants; summaries or full texts of lectures; and mimeographed or printed reports of Graduate Schools, conferences and courses. (Unfortunately, these archives are not complete owing to flooding in the library.) There is also some Bossey material in the WCC archives in Geneva.

In the early 1980s *Hans-Heinrich Wolf* started to write a history of Bossey. Both his unfinished draft in German and the source material gathered for it were used in writing the present history.

During the early period, reports on the life and work of Bossey were often published in the periodicals *Laymen's Work* (1951-55) and *Laity* (1956-68). Also *The Ecumenical Review* (since 1948), *Study Encounter* (1965-76) and *Ministerial Formation* (since 1978) have occasionally published material from Bossey. For the general ecumenical context see *Dictionary of the Ecumenical Movement*, Geneva, WCC, 1991, and *A History of the Ecumenical Movement*, vols I and II, Geneva, WCC, 1993.

For the history of the domain of Bossey and the early periods of the Institute see:

Guillaume Fatio, *Céligny: commune genevoise*, Céligny, 1949, pp.3ff.,314f.,337-56.

François Bucher, *Notre-Dame de Bonmont*, Band VII der Berner Schriften zur Kunst, Bern, 1957.

Jacques Vincent, *La belle Mademoiselle Lange*, Paris, 1932, pp.183-282 (a sketch of life at Bossey in the early 19th century).

Hendrik Kraemer, "L'Eglise chrétienne dans la crise mondiale", inaugural lecture, October 1946, *Cahiers de l'Institut œcuménique*, no. 1, Geneva, 1946. From issue no. 3 onwards this series of early Bossey publications was continued in English with the title *Papers of the Ecumenical Institute*.

Bossey: Two Vignettes from the Early Years, with contributions of
Willem A. Visser 't Hooft and Suzanne de Diétrich, Bossey, 1981.
Arnold Mobbs, *Les origines et les premières années de l'Institut
œcuménique de Bossey*, Bossey, 1983.

Reports of meetings

Reports of almost all Bossey meetings are in the Bossey archives,
and many are also in the library of the Ecumenical Centre in Geneva.
The following is only a selection, listing mainly interdisciplinary
conferences (the date of the conference is in brackets). Some of these
reports also appeared in French and German; here only the English
version (if it exists) is given.

"Educateurs chrétiens" (July-August 1947), *Cahiers de l'Institut
œcuménique*, no. 2, Geneva, 1947.

"Professional Life as Christian Vocation" (1947-48), *Papers of the
Ecumenical Institute*, no. 3, Geneva, 1948.

"Contributions to a Christian Social Ethics" (April 1948), *Papers of
the Ecumenical Institute*, no. 4, Geneva, 1949.

"On the Meaning of History" (August 1949), *Papers of the Ecumenical Institute*, no. 5, Geneva, 1949.

"Christianity and Social Work" (July 1951), *Laymen's Work*, no. 4,
1952.

"Bible and Ecumenism" (September 1955), *The Student World*,
1956.

"The Training of the Laity for Their Ministry in the World" (April
1956), *Laity*, no. 2, 1956.

"The Missionary Church in the East and the West" (June 1958),
London, 1959.

"The Meaning of the Secular" (September 1959), mimeographed,
Bossey, 1959.

"Ecumenics and Ecumenical Theology" (August 1960), mimeographed, Bossey, 1960.

"Stewardship — an Ecumenical Confrontation" (August/September
1961), *Laity*, no. 12, 1961; full report, New York, 1961.

"Tenth Anniversary of the Graduate School of Ecumenical Studies",
The Ecumenical Review, 14, 1, 1961.

"The Impact of Secondary Education on Young People" (March-April
1962), Geneva, 1962.

"Christians in Power Structures" (May 1962), *Laity*, no. 14, 1962.

"Towards a Christian Attitude to Money" (August/September 1965), *Laity*, no. 21, 1966.

"The Common Nature of Mental Illness and Health" (April 1966), *Study Encounter*, 1966.

"Human Engineering and Christian Growth" (August 1966), mimeographed, Bossey, 1966.

"The Teaching of Practical Theology" (August 1967), mimeographed, Bossey, 1967.

"Experiments with Man" (September 1968), *WCC Studies*, Geneva, 1969.

"Participation in Industry" (April 1969), *Study Encounter*, 1969.

"Ecclesiastical Decisions: A Test Case for the Ecumenical Movement" (June 1969), *Study Encounter*, 1969.

"Conflict, Violence and Peace" (July 1969), *WCC Studies*, Geneva, 1970.

"Man, the Steward of Power" (August 1969), mimeographed, Bossey, 1969.

"Penal Policies" (June 1970), mimeographed, Bossey, 1970.

"The Wisdom of the Body" (August 1970), mimeographed, Bossey, 1970.

"Sports in a Christian Perspective" (August 1970), mimeographed, Bossey, 1970.

"Industrial Production" (May 1971), mimeographed, Bossey, 1971.

"The Bible in Our Ministry" (June 1971), *The Ecumenical Review*, 23, 4, 1971.

"Dogmatic or Contextual Theology" (August 1971), mimeographed, Bossey, 1972.

"Doctrine and Change" (June 1972), mimeographed, Bossey, 1972.

"The Price of Progress" (April 1973), mimeographed, Bossey, 1973.

"The Creation of a New Man" (September 1973), mimeographed, Bossey, 1973.

"Power and Property in the Use of World Resources" (April 1974), mimeographed, Bossey, 1974.

"Doing Theology Today" (three consultations 1972-74), Mysore, 1976.

"The Church in Search of Community Life" (June-July 1974), mimeographed, Bossey, 1974.

"Human Identity in Nature, Science and Society" (April 1975), Bossey, 1975.

"Prophetic Vocation in the New Testament and Today" (September 1975), Leiden, 1977.

"Self-reliance and Solidarity in the Quest for International Justice" (April 1976), Part I: Geneva, 1976; Part II: Bossey, 1977.

"African and Asian Contributions to Contemporary Theology" (June 1976), Bossey, 1977.

"Spirituality and Ecumenism" (June-July 1976), Bossey, 1976.

"Confessing Christ in Different Cultures" (July 1977), Bossey, 1977.

"The Gospel and International Life" (July 1977), Bossey, 1977.

"Christian and Jewish Dialogue on Man" (March 1978), Bossey, 1980.

"Indigenous Theology and the Universal Church" (June 1978), Bossey, 1979.

"The Healing Ministry of the Church" (June-July 1979), mimeographed, Bossey/Geneva, 1979.

"Signs and Symbols in the Communication of the Gospel" (April 1981), Bossey, 1981.

"The Truth Shall Make You Free" (July 1981), Bossey, 1981.

"Education for Effective Ecumenism" (June 1982), mimeographed, Geneva, 1982.

"Confessing Jesus Christ Today" (March 1984), Bossey, 1984.

"Women in Church Leadership" (June 1986), Bossey, 1987.

"The Teaching of Ecumenics" (July 1986), Geneva, 1987.

"Christianity and Culture: 40 Years of the Ecumenical Institute" (January 1967), *The Ecumenical Review*, 39, 2, 1987.

"The Search for New Community" (May 1987), Geneva, 1989.

"Partnership in Ecumenical Leadership Formation" (September 1989), mimeographed, Bossey, 1989.

"God Has Called Us: Ecumenical Workshop for Women Theological Educators" (May 1991), Geneva, 1994.

"Regards sur l'Orthodoxie" (April 1992), mimeographed, Bossey, 1993.

"Communication Education" (April-May 1992), *Ministerial Formation*, 58, 1992.

"Spectrum of Ministry" (July 1992), *Ministerial Formation*, 60, 1993.

"Sustainable Growth — A Contradiction in Terms? Visser 't Hooft Memorial Consultation" (June 1993), Geneva, 1993.

"Women's Visions: Theological Reflection, Celebration, Action" (May 1994), Geneva, 1995.

Ecumenical dissertations

In connection with the Graduate School the following seven ecumenical doctoral dissertions were written:

Hellmut Rosin, "The Lord Is God: The Translation of Divine Names and the Missionary Calling of the Church", Geneva, 1955.

Robert Tobias, "Communist-Christian Encounter in East Europe: 1917-1951", Geneva, 1956.

Richard C. Smith, "A Critical Evaluation of Industrial Evengelism", Geneva, 1959.

Hans-Ruedi Weber, "Asia and the Ecumenical Movement: 1895-1961", London, 1966.

Armin Boyens, "Ökumenische Bewegung und Bekenntniskirche in Deutschland: 1933 bis Kriegsausbruch in 1939", Munich, 1969.

Geoffrey Wainwright, "Eucharist and Eschatology", Geneva, 1971.

Raymond Pelly, "The Spirit, the Church and the Churches", Geneva, 1971.

Christine Baron, "Abendmahlsgemeinschaft als eschatologisches Problem", Munster, 1975.

Johannes Thomas Hörnig, "Mission und Einheit: Geschichte und Theologie der amerikanischen Sonntagsschulbewegung", Maulbronn, 1991.

Index of Persons

What is ecumenism?

How can ecumenism be taught?

How is it related to the idea of God? / to humanities' spiritual quest? - search for meaning, purpose, fulfilment, life.? / for justice, community?

What is meant by history here?

Can we deconstruct "ecumenism"? - what is the genealogy of the institute at Bossey? What is the debate, the specifics, the actuality?

vii - ecumenism as renewal.
  - growing together for new insights into how to live a fuller life:

vii the success of ecumenism was its capacity to find new life by many world-wide - but did it?

4 - ecumenism as pain :- Marriage failure.

Building human community through repentance and renewal.

19 - shift from Barthianism to liberation - Visser't Hooft to Raiser - coincide gestes world wide vision.

23 - ecumenism : staying together while disagreeing -

35 : Ecumenism = correct thought ; ch Hist : lay ministry
with bible study.

38-40 + thought : emphasis on lay people : lay vocation - cf.
Oldh biog. 11, 56 lay being as ecumen histy.
cf 64 re. Weber.

51 The pickerns of ecumerism : A Part of the graduate school
Program : what steps to buildg of world community a the
renewal of the churches.

72 studying ecumenical themes related to WCC.

74 fieldwork projects : — a diff type of ecumen study.

76 A. Th. van Leeuwen : Christianity in World History.
[Harry Cox : Type on Fire]

90 changing notions of ecumenism — from interconfessional to
intercultural & ethical.
+ 93 with whith,

100 Post - Nairobi rethinking and defense of Assay.
+ 101 new aims

101 ecumenism as interconfessional a intercultural

103 ecumenism as drg θ in an ecumenical context
: now θ is ecumenism.

106 ecumenism : as the experience of living & being together.

107 (+ 104) shift for world centred to church centred work.

126 Basis WCC chgd 1961

125/126 diff understandigs and definitions of ecumen ✳
with reference ad suive doremts.